A Different Way Of Being

By Zen Garcia

SANDI—

GLAD YOUR DOING

SO WELL BROTHER. IT

A Different Way Of Being

HAS BEEN LONG THAT

By Zen

WE'VE HAD CHANCE

TO HANG OUT. LET'S

MAKE A POINT TO

GET TOGETHER.

PEACE

ZEN

Dedicated to the memory of Justin Dart

-Tom Olin

Get involved
in politics
as if
your life
depended on it,
because
it does.

—Justin Dart

Contents

Chapter 3 - The Beautiful People

Chapter 4 – Can't Find My Way Home

Chapter 5 – Forever Moments

Chapter 6 - We Shall Overcome

Chapter 7 – Enduring Tragedy

Chapter 8 - Endeavor Freedom

Chapter 9 – Reality Check

Chapter 10 - The World Stands Still

Chapter 11 - Bahamas Journal

-Tom Olin

Foreword

As someone who's been disabled and used a wheelchair for over 30 years, Zen's poems remind me of the pain, joy, growth and change I've experienced in times of my life when I've done a lot of soul searching, getting in touch with faith and God. Life is a journey and 'A Different Way Of Being' is an insightful diary of one man's will to reclaim self, "more found in my wheelchair than I ever was lost and walking around". Zen says two significant things must occur in life. "Truth has to be realized and love has to be lived." Zen Garcia is a rare mix, a gifted poet, passionate activist, and father at 33 years of age. Advocacy had to become a large part of Zen's lifestyle, "a part of his fate." He's had his ('Reality Check') and realized "life deserves more than idle conscious." Clearly his parents, "who bear the brunt of hurt" have played a major role in assisting him this far.

Disability happens daily and really is only as big a deal as you make it. It's a natural consequence of interacting with our environment. It teaches us and those around, not to take things for granted, and to re-evaluate what is important in life and living. It allows us to know that there is more than one way to do things. Most importantly we learn disability isn't the problem; attitudes, myths, perceptions and prejudice are, as Zen writes, 'Accept Me for Who I Am." When we fight who we are, we resist and fear change, getting used to routine which leave us in stagnation. Unfortunately, lethargy can become a way of life for many post-disability.

The more stress accumulates, the more our conscious narrows and we conform to not do anything at all about the ways we are and the life we have been 'fated' to live. Complacency can be in large part to doubts about self and lack of confidence, trust in who we think we can become. Disability can change us for better if we allow it; all we need is a map. 'A Different Way Of Being' is that map.

Few institutions know much about the disability rights movement and what's going on now. We are in process of redefining problems and issues. We are changing attitudes declaring pity as wrong. The independent living movement seeks to broaden visions of empowerment to individuals who need assistance in their daily living; forcing people to focus on relationships and less on autonomy, independence in tasks and skills. Instead of self-independence, survival depends on inter-dependence, a paradigm of we together can do it, we can cooperate; we can combine our talents and abilities and create something greater. Life is about connections. It is about how to get along, how to understand others, and how to forge successful relationships. In a broader sense, it is about community, about working with others to make a life and make a difference. 'A Different Way Of Being' through Zen's life illustrates that and if nothing else that we can as a group, as a collective, as a force create change improving the lives of us all. "The people united will never be defeated."

- Mark Johnson

XIV

A Different Way Of Being

I've lived a charmed life blessed to do the many
things I've come to know over the years, brought up
by parents kind enough to want to spoil me with all
they never grew up with. Fate fortuned I would
never have to struggle hard to acquire meal, clothes,
or comfortable lodging. They worked incessantly,
disciplined themselves all their lives, living
honestly, and pushing for all they'd acquired. I love
them for their grand example and gracious love, for
always accepting me for who I am.

Physical disability though a challenged endeavor is
by no means the end of opportunistic living.
Everyone will experience obstacle to daily routine.
Even saints have limitations, challenges to temper
lesson in this world. Breaking my neck was a wake
up call, a slap in the face, what are you up to when
you know where you should be leading moment
from here. Now I feel fortunate to have clear
understanding on what I should do with what time I
have in this realm remaining.

Whether with or without disability, we have choice
only to live fully in instance, or not. All are getting
older fading moment with no promise of future
morrow. No moment to waste, no second to lose,
this is first and last each moment for me and I
cannot hope to convey any greater message than
live every moment as if it is all you have, no other
possibility left in this Earthwalk. Life has no
ordinary occurrence, and deserves more than idle
conscious.

Disability like forced meditation, challenges soul to find, locate something authentic outside of what people term 'normal' decree. Moments of gauche tragedy force us to question belief systems, observance to what we consider real, what truly matters, and which issues in life hold significance. Everyone at some time in life will face moments one is unsure of surviving; when breathe is stolen, tears fountain like rain, pain like no words can describe owns your being. It's part of the process.

We can easily spend lifetimes wandering entertained by outside persuasion, evading center until finally moment compromises invulnerability, and the body nearing mortality experiences the beyond, and in that instance we question the relevance of life choices and other possibilities. Reality checks are death reminding us there is really not enough time to do everything you want, so you do what you can with what time you have now; weighing that some things are hardly worth holding on to.

When life is flashing before ones eyes, chaos ruling emotions touch on desperate; in that moment all one wants is a second chance. Disability for many is that second chance and we must make the most of it. I know it is difficult to understand when all one wants is somewhere to hide, to be alone, to stop the flood of outside stimuli, and people entering room saying everything's going to be alright. I've been there, unable to escape or hide; I lay there watching, witnessing the unfolding before me unsure of what was next and where to from here.

This is the road less traveled, but traveled still and boldly, courageously, beautifully by some. All people have issues, things they're working on to determine self-definition. Everyone at sometime will wonder- how do I get past the first gate to the darkness beyond? How do I satisfy soul purpose in this broken state of body? Always right where we need be, don't beat yourself up with what may have been, had you done something different. That was then this is now. Now is happening before you inviting you into its grasp.

Unsuspectingly thrown into strange world, forced to redefine life and schedule; I pray you find peace quickly these moments of initial shattering and that some semblance of pleasure returns to your living. Families, friends, neighbors, associates, all those around will be hugely impacted, especially in beginning when one learns how much paralysis or disability affects every aspect of life. Remember then, everyone has barriers placed before them in life, birth gives us that privilege. Barriers hold some for some time, keeping us from going further, but at some point all must make decision to simply go on; accepting to make the best of situation.

My hope with this work is save you some of the heartache and pain, associated with initiation into spinal cord injury especially quadriplegia. I endear to show you that there is light at the end of the tunnel and if you can't crawl to get there, do as Mark said find someone to share struggle along way. Interdependence and cooperation is a huge part of this new way of being.

In sharing hope, we can help one another dissipate some of the pain and frustration disability can breed. May disability become for you like it is now for me, just 'A Different Way Of Being.' May this book settle some of the carnage, associated to enduring great loss. Those of you overwhelmed in the deepest depression, trust I have been there and have survived beautifully. Getting to where I am now is process. If you are at beginning now trudge on. Having gone through it myself, these poems reflect my evolution through very real moments of human challenge, where fate contends live anew in wake of past experience.

Disability has evolved me through some very intense moments, teaching me lessons of patience and perseverance that demanded my slowing down, reevaluating life, and reassessing living. Determination will decide if you can find comfort in similar circumstance. Be where you feel you are and let no other dictate where you feel you need to be. Take your time in transformation. Arctic butterflies take years to cocoon their wings. You will develop your own way. This road is but an extension of a branch leading us all to the same place. Namaste.

Zen Garcia 10-14-2002 Injured 09-24-1994

A man seeking lost paradise
may seem a fool
to those
who have never
sought the other world

-Jim Morrison

Chapter 1 – Wounded Limbs

-Heather Hays

I don't believe it's all important to be
what our culture calls "optimal."
Getting old isn't easy
for a lot of us.
Neither is living,
neither is dying.
We struggle against the inevitable
and we all suffer because of it.
We have to find
another way to look
at the whole process
of being born, growing old,
changing, and dying,
some kind of perspective
that might allow us
to deal with what we perceive
as big obstacles
without having to be dragged
through the drama.
It really helps to understand
that we have something,
that we are something,
which is unchangeable,
beautiful, completely aware,
and continues no matter what.

-Ram Dass

Strange Day

Cool fall settles in with fresh zephyr
dawn beats away Ancient night
reflecting stained glass morning

Eager for majestic day
awaiting Brenda to start morning routine
trio of cats stretched across dormant legs

Seems just a reverie away 1994
studying massage at Heartwood
Institute of Healing Arts
East of Garberville
nestled in the emerald triangle
near Eureka and Trinidad
200 miles north of San Francisco
on the Mendocino fault
near the Redwood valleys
of Northern California

Clouds thick with the cool dawn
the sun cleared skies by 11 a.m.
mornings consisted of hiking
to mountain peak for twilight yoga with Gayna
followed by greeting sun with Michael in Tai-Chi
then Polarity class with Bruce
learning fundamentals of energy

Rumor on campus
some heard that the Grateful Dead
would play acoustic at the Warfield
as the Warlocks for those propitious to attend

Noon we snacked a quick organic feast
then caught ride with Gypsy
in a purple beat-up old VW van
easy trekking canyon cliffs
snaking desolate roads to highway 101
40 miles from Pacific Coast 1
just south of the Valley of Giants
where Redwoods stand primordial lofty proud

About 30 minutes into the descent
just after reaching paved roads
smoked out brakes surrendered grip to gravity
momentum gave-way to extreme acceleration

Increasing velocity rapidly loosing control
road disappearing to surrounding blur
there was no way to halt what was to come
nowhere to go nowhere to run

A few minutes turned into long centuries
terror animating moments
rubber trying to cleave to road
as speed gathered shooting us
sideways off graveyard cliffs

In death lunge there was just enough time
to realize space
before trees snapped limbs crackled
as we caved ridge in meteoric crash

Mountain unmoving my body puddle to ground
squashed in instant Jell-O smash
head snapped back in whiplash fashion

Carrie screamed my arm my arm
O, God... my arm
someone please help
then silence overcame panic moments

I knew something was certainly wrong
I tried to get up to run
to reach escape before the van exploded

Unresponsive my body lay
collapsed heavy in pain
arms swaying when I try to move
uncontrollably like limbs of trees
pushed by the wind's own interest

Loosing consciousness
inclination to breathe
body in despair
vision lost ears ringing
uncertain void stealing soul to new flight

Thinking Chinese

Laid up shattered on hospital bed
baffled by current circumstance
no retort TV for comfort/friend

Bewilderment I came to
in I.C.U. senses reeling feeling extremes
in temperatures pain awkward upheaval

3 times Flat-line death prevailing
asphyxiation pneumonia clogged breath

Weeks gone I can't even recall
screws drilled into skull
stabilizing the halo aligning my neck

Doctors backed by med school degrees
intruded morning sleep
making routine rounds
condemning me with callous word
to never walk again

'This is how it was going to be'
paralysis living with disability
dependent on monster wheelchair
help dressing bathing using bathroom

As quick as they came they left
leaving me racked in pain
wishing for a hole to hide
where nobody could touch me or see me
where all the noise and drama
would just disappear

5

They think they know disability
because of expensive degrees
years of college education
advising and then walking out

I wanted a hammer to crush skulls
shatter spines
this is paralysis
no walking out

They psychiatrist says I'm depressed
well damn it man
I just broke my fricken neck
what do you expect?

Get out get out leave me alone
your books can't explain
what I'm going through
don't feed me your intellectual opinion
or professional revelation

Go charge your 150 bucks an hour
to Medicaid but please
spare me the lame explanations

I'm screaming inside
scared out of my wits
unsure what next to do
what can I do?

Just turn off the light as you go
and shut the door
as you leave

Get up get up I say
but my body won't listen
leaving me stranded in bed alone
having pissed on myself
as if I'm thinking Chinese

**I have been very near
the Gates of Death
& have returned
very weak & an Old Man
feeble & tottering,
but not in Spirit & Life
not in The Real Man
The Imagination which Liveth for Ever.
In that I am stronger & stronger
as this Foolish Body decays.**

-William Blake

For Mom and Dad

Kind loving gentle soul parents
nothing but love for you

I apologize for my misgivings
for pushing further
than most need to go alone

I'm so sorry
you had to fly to California
to be by my side
see me so utterly broken
plugged by needles and tubes
so many machines surrounding
as death ruled my world

I struggled for life breath
as you paced waiting rooms
for news and chance reconciliation
crawled from hell & high mountain
when all was darkness cold
promise only of more suffering more pain

Light hurt sound anguishing
everything discomfort
sleep evaded
I couldn't fathom survival this way

But you pushed me
willed me to try and make it
through confused circumstance
disability intruding routine

Life balanced precariously
on dancing blip of green line
trachea regulated ventilator air
feeding tube for liquid goop

My body once so tone
shriveled away
bones poking through
you provided what comfort you could
resigning to love me
in whatever way was possible

Family is one of those sacred words
whose meaning is not a birthright
but evolved through situation

It must be nurtured by lesson
celebrated by story
having been granted special provision
ultimate struggle
and in some instances seeming tragedy

Thank you both so much
I love you in ways
words could never reveal

Wounded Limbs

My friend & nurse Ellen
throws sunflower seeds out on the ground
as soon as she is done
all the animals come around

Families of cardinals doves
6 squirrels & a couple of jays
here as the sun rises
they stay until the evening of every day

The older cardinals fly in first
whistle to young waiting in the tree
with brief hesitation children fly down
knowing its okay to feed

One of the Jays larger than the rest
chases the other birds away
the doves are the only to hold ground
& if their around the others will stay

Over time I see their changes
seasons of growth to life outside
still recently broken I'm shattered
unsure of what I might write

September 24 of 1994
hitchhiking our van careened off a hill
now May of 1995 a new year
and I'm still deciding how I feel

-

We lost our brakes on a mountain in Cali
plunged 85 feet to the ground
I tried to get up realized then
I was paralyzed from neck down

After tragedy one can easily give up
lose hope of gathering any faith
seems there's nothing left to live for
do I even have the strength?

Time to waste away
give up now that I can no longer move
A brief moment of tragedy left me
with what seems nothing more to lose

In a dream I dreamt I walked away
freed from the prison of my bed
I was able to move in full capacity
unlike all those doctors said

I went to find a nurse shocking her
everyone was fully surprised
How could I step away from this
great tragedy in my life

It was then that I woke up
still unable to move
the joy in my heart dissipated
depression ensued

Hopelessly suicidal at first
my mind felt betrayed
though I always felt close to Spirit
motionless here I lay

Feeling life to be over
better I should die nothing could I do
Couldn't wipe away tears I cry
couldn't run I couldn't move

Couldn't scratch my head
or even blow my nose
Couldn't feed myself
or put on my own clothes

Never had I contended before
how people became paralyzed
& what that exactly meant for them
so different in daily life

How things can drastically change
in the wind of just one breathe
How it seems that we walk always
one moment away from death

It's taken me nine very long months
to get my head kind of straight
For me to even want to begin to deal
with this strange twist in my fate

The greatest struggle now
gather what's left of the unbroken
quiet the crazy mind of thoughts
associated with being broken

This is the longest journey I've ever wandered
hardest role I've had to play
Definitely the strangest trial I had to bear
in what is the weirdest quirk of fate

Old friends disappear unable to cope
with friendship in this way
But there are newer friends to replace
those who run away

Must place emphasis on what's eternal
a life in the immortal journey of soul
Keep it all in perspective
watch it all unfold

Waiting Room Families

Unable to cope
with weird situations
scattered thoughts
that cross their minds
I feel compassion for those parents
crying to pass the time

Seeing their children broken
hanging on a whim
Facing dire circumstance
chances nil to slim

Peace to you in nights you try to sleep
exhausted but still awake
wishing there was something you could do
anything but just wait
Grieving hearts painfully sad
a million questions to the Lord
I say to you never doubt the path unfolding
for those whose destiny seems strange reward

Remember how to laugh
and try not to worry excessively too much
Watch your own health rest and nap
slow down your pace no rush
Don't waste all your moments
wishing it the way things were before
That's all past history now
those realities exist no more

Great Spirit bless the parents of this world
who bear the brunt of hurt
So difficult is it for them
having to do all the work

Bless us Great Mystery with smile
a gesture of your grace
So we may be strong in hope
in the trials we now face

My mother my father
no greater blessing there could be
The strange bond we now have
stemming from this injury

15

Condescending Facade

"What's wrong?" "How did it happen?"
"I'm sorry. You'll get better one day."
Judged and I'd never even met them before

My mom a Deacon in her church
was told by members of the congregation
that I must have been engaged in sinful living
for me to be so struck down

In order that I might walk again
it was imperative that I be saved
in accordance to the ways
and beliefs of her Church
otherwise remain 'unworthy'
of the Lord's consolation

They said if I prayed enough
and deserved it
everything would be fine
that God would redeem
my rampant living

She believed
which made it all the worse

Many from the congregation came to see me
in the hospital
praying over me preaching
while I huddle away cold
drowning in blankets
racked in horrific pain

I didn't want to see the overhead light
much less the strange faces of people
thinking me an obvious sinner

There could be no hell
worse than this
sense disorientation
piercing agony like I'd never known before

They didn't know of my past
that I'd done ceremony
in the desert alone
fasting and praying
inviting Spirit to circle

They assumed I needed to be saved
could they believe everybody in hospital a sinner?

I've experienced incredible 'religious' moments
circumstance indescribable
to nonchalant conversation

They'd never understand telling me
'their way is the only way'
the rest would burn in hell

They said I must accept
they know what's right

I said "Hey, hey let's skip the sermon,
speak from the heart
see where Spirit leads conversation"

17

"You're not the only ones
doing the work

Let's share the lessons life imposes
screw squabbling over differences
in language or idea

The same rain that feeds the Earth
showers all people without regard

Let's talk heart to heart
not war over belief systems
but seek to reunite
the separation causing
your judgment of my condition"

Crippled Saints

We went to the movies
6 of us
3 walking 3 in chairs

Freezing though the sun shone bright
we saw "Powder" & sprinkled tears

Racing back to catch the sunset
night beat us home
drinking spiced cider
I warmed enough to write this poem

Powder offered his gift
to those unabashed by his looks

Bringer of dawn
he spread cryptic moments
on dying gardens in need of summer roses

How true for so many
wearing the mask of disability
souls eclipsed by passing fates

Treasures to bring
secrets to share
they pass us by
totally unaware
of the jewels
lining our pockets

One day all the stories
will have been written
all the roles played
the curtain will go up
& like old times
we'll create thoughts
for which are no words

Newly disabled
rediscovering the joys of life
I am what Spirit intends for me to be
stronger even with new promises to keep
& reason to keep them

Life as a quad is not so bad
just different
being a Leo
I always thrive on being center attention

The initial loss of freedom
movement & control
left broken questions
in a shaken mind
unsure of life
with such peculiarly quiet
though sometimes lively limbs

Over it
I tend to see myself now
as somewhat of a King
though I do what I can
some things I can't do
I don't mind not doing at all

No less human being disabled
still living passionately
growing accustomed
to the new look
in a stranger's eye

Where once looks of hunger prevailed
now looks of wonder reveal
curious discretion

The soul behind the mask
is always free to dream

Once rippling washboard abs
feet and fists
like hammers of lightning
able to heal or hurt
activate or alleviate pain

The body I so endearingly
stretched and shaped
formed from blood sweat and tears
through thousands of hours
beating away at unforgiving bags
journeys to other dojos to fight their best

Even if I knew
I'd do it all again

So what if my stomach swells
and my hips widen
paralyzed what's your excuse?

So I'll go through this life allowing
pretty nurses to give aid
comfort in awkward instances

Intimacy certain
humor a must
one life obliging
over zealous individuals
looking for opportunity to lend
an always appreciated hand

No better way to meet a friend
than in asking for help
with a door

A Different Way of Being

Another day passes yielding to night
candles fade cascades to shade
Keenest silence ample time to write
I'm recollecting events decisions
that I've made

Extremely weird
this different way of being
so much time to entertain thought
Almost used to waking
in this weird kind of dream
unsure still
what it is I'm being taught

What of this time
marred by natural disasters
the many predicaments testing our race
It is a time for each of us to master
conditions we are in
struggles we now must face

Misunderstood the weird quirks of fate
in battle who decides
which of us should fall?
Why some die immediately some to wait
why them why us why any at all

Speculation about life
how we ever came to be
seeking answers to questions unknown
Here I am pondering improbability
knowing some lessons all must face alone

There must be reason to endure
something to thrust want to survive
Life key enchanting its allure
the most awesome blessing just to be alive

Each carries rocks
though some carry boulders
each a cross a burden to bear
Some are like Atlas
the world on their shoulders
carrying more than what seems fair share

Sometimes it's hard to confront pain
endure sorrows felt in heart
Sometimes our own thinking
drives us insane
the faith we struggled to gain falling apart

Scales are weighed measured in the end
though we live this moment
struggling right now
We'll be together forever all of us again
the suffering of our souls
redeemed somehow

We must pleasure in simple presence
consciousness in this enchanted world
sun dawning smile of spring flowers
Like the innocence of young boy or little girl
delighted with life
every second of every hour

Sensory satisfaction is pleasure for soul
everything new we have again chance to do
Never surrender dreams or the struggle for goals
hold fast to faith
angel grace will pull us through

The moment's effect entrances mind
a miracle every scene that passes
life is but a dream
& dreams fade with time
like hammers of lightning
happening in short flashes

Such a blessing to be alive
part of the creation
thank & praise the Creator
Each moment we have of life
each rising day falling night
each memory is
another sunset to savor

Challenged Existence
-For Beth Tumlin and Catherine Stefanavage

Parents of children with disability
are pushed to experience
the kind of unconditional love
that life in traditional mode
never gives challenge to know

Those that make it
facing uncertain circumstance
battling every prejudice
label and expectation
bless you
your commitment will be your reward

You will know parenting
in ways most are never
determined to know
or chance to receive

Love that withstood withstands
giving definition
worthy of its stature

Love we've yet to realize
the propensity of the word
sort of like All or One
holding everything
in one syllabic embrace

He explained to me then the intricacies of choice. He said that choice, for warrior-travelers, was not really the act of choosing, but rather the act of acquiescing elegantly to the solicitations of infinity.

"Infinity chooses," he said "The art of the warrior-traveler is to have the ability to move with the slightest insinuation, the art of acquiescing to every command of infinity.

For this, a warrior-traveler needs prowess, strength, and above everything else, sobriety. All those three put together give, as a result, elegance!"

- Carlos Castaneda

Chapter 2 –Reclaiming Self

-Dominic Ottaviano

There is a big difference
between being lonely
and being alone.
Loneliness is an affair of the ego.
Being alone
can be a moment for the soul.
It is necessary
to be alone
to have the time
to be quiet,
to meditate,
to get to know ourselves.
The soul
cannot grow into awareness
if the ego
keeps us busy
with other people, activities,
or worrying about
how lonely we are.
Being alone
is a great opportunity
to define
who we truly are.

-Ram Dass

Further Faster

All I ever wanted to do was play
stomp mud puddles and sluicing rains
lay face-down in the dirt
and watch ants crawl

Who knew we'd spend so many years
nurturing identity
trying to relate self to world
make sense of what we saw on TV

When 18 and coming of age
I remember chasing rampant upheaval
open to all plausible possibility
avail anything once
burn candle from both ends
get further faster

Lucky to have endured those years
some of us are quirked along the way
broken by fate
realizing frailty too late

Some falter completely
pushing too hard
dying ignorant innocent
falling to casualty
relinquishing chance to attest adulthood
with wisdom of ascending years

Some are given option
to grant different treason
go about life in new way

Art saved me from further courting travesty
occupying time with prose and sketches
paper and pen to guide ruse

I read choice literature
spied film and visual art
studying the work of historic masters
fancied creating imaginative works
opinions and words for them
also surviving awkward oblivion
given option to understand
chance differently

There must be some legacy to remind
warn others of the dangers
of pushing too far
or giving up
when back is against the wall

Gifted Tongue

Early morning at Options Cottage
Roosevelt Warm Springs
Institute for Rehabilitation

Brushing my teeth
a visiting nurse enters my room
carrying a book I had been reading
'Dreamtime & Inner Space"
explaining significance of dreams
to tribal culture
and shamanic interpretation

She said are you saved
aren't you afraid of hell
be ye aware of devil spirits
that roam earthly halls
in search of loathing souls
believe & receive
the gift of tongues

She then babbled some incoherent dialect
trying to prove to me
she had righteous gift
mixafrixaplixa
murphaklumprukfumkut

I rinsed my mouth out
looking directly into her eye and said
you know not me
or gifts I bring world
I speak in poems

Unbridled Passion

Caught up in thinking
questioning what it is I want to say
Speaking to you last night
stranded me this way
Sleep evaded head spinning
wandering with my thoughts
Querying what the future holds
battles I've already fought
How can I say without tainting
words heavy on my heart
How can I reveal my feelings to you
without changing what they are
Will these circumstances fade you
to hide or leave feelings unsaid
Will you feel as deeply as I
words that you've just read

I left you in California
would see you when Fall Tour came around
meet you in Boston
hang out with you in your town
Be with you to see the Dead
6 shows in 7 nights
It would have been so fricken cool
nothing could have been more right
Together embrace the Dead
get that feeling of coming home
Another night celebrating with the Boys
you and I alone
then there was the accident & Jerry passed away
Suddenly everything
was halted by strange delay

I remember when I was hurting most
your voice conferred life to my ears
Like some distant Angel ghost
out of nowhere your calls appeared
At that time I couldn't speak
barely hearing what people say
A step away from passing
looming death just a breath away
Then they flew me to Shepherd
finally thoughts with you over phone
You gave me comfort in my plight
sharing pain I held alone

I opened up to you told you things
when all I wanted was to hide
I revealed to you jumbled thoughts
I had buried deep inside
So much had changed would it even matter
The condition I've found myself in
like a puzzle broken pieces scattered
Crushed like volcanic dust
blown on frenzied winds
Not wanting to be where I am
I have to sort out pieces of self again
So weird to feel feelings
with a body that's unfeeling
Sorting through scattered thoughts
needing great healing

It's a different way of being
that I learn from everyday
A lesson of patience I walk
in the new role that I play

Spared for whatever reason
yet defined I guess we'll see
Can't help thinking this is just another part
of the strangest destiny

So this is my first day
kicking it at Warm Springs
Another day scripting thoughts
praise to the Creator
of all our dreams

The Book Of Tours

For 4 years I frequented interstate corridors
chasing lines fading to distant horizon

The road fed my desire
lending freedom to always new dream
where I remain anonymous
to any past adhered by others

I was whatever I wanted to be
every moment filled mystery
an exciting book never knowing
next page or scene

Like 'Fear And Loathing'
no story could equal
or resemble the beautiful madness
I found chasing The Grateful Dead
from city to city
state to state

Life was dreamy
chancing fate and fortune friends
in seek of carnival pleasure

Wake with carnation sunrise
race sun to westward horizon
dead red crash and burn
fading light caressing seas

Poems could never convey the experience fully
these lines celebrate those moments
Jerry and the Boys years of performance magic

Conjuring ancient feeling to assembly
opening gateway invitation
for those willing to assume pursuit
having learned some kind of something
hosting all those acid tests years ago

Scattered now the dust settled
The sage seeks freedom from desire
He does not collect precious things
He learns not to hold on to ideas
He brings others back to what they have lost

-Lao Tzu

Muse Lead

We need inspiration
to touch us hold us grip us in awe
if but for a second
leaving us intrigued

No limitations
I am not confined
by others expectation

I will be the miracle in me
I will be what they've yet to see
I will be he
defining new prophecy
riddled by something grander
greater more powerful beautiful
than our understandings
of self defined by society

Disability forces redefining
self and situation
I am found in my wheelchair
among those lost and walking around

New day promises
possible experience
appealing soul to ever stranger adventure
the hope of future fantasy
moments burned to mind
her eyes in parading glow

Faded Years

I hope life finds you well son
into myriad things
as a child bordering teen should be

I wish I knew moments with you
what passions your life now

Wish I could encourage your evolution
things you love to do
share techniques of carting girls' interest

I am sure you are aided
nurtured by those around
Stacy as always holding you dear

I ask myself all the time
what would be the best way
to communicate with and know you now
without causing more controversy
or extending dissent

I promised your mother
jealous step father
to leave your new family dynamics alone

We never spoke to you about it
or asked you your opinion
you were so young
just in the line of fire

What did you really think of me
did you think of me at all

I don't know anything about your life now
this poem like others
another shot in the dark
get a few words down
so that you know one day when we meet again
you were are in my mind all the time
you are my heart my soul
and I give regard to you always

I will send these words await reply
hoping to one day know instead of imagine
your passions things you emphasize
in your life wandering

Justin I love you just so you know
I apologize again for everything I did
didn't do that continues our distance

I offer prayers for you in your becoming
hoping your lessons in this life
be pleasant rewarding as pain-free as possible

I know you will be a blessing to the world
a light for others seeking way
tell your Mom
I always think of her with fine regard

We were too young to understand
incapable of handling
love in such fragile circumstance

She is a fine woman
I couldn't have picked one better
to mother my child

Between Two Worlds

Pastel colors swirl in motion
I give thanks for life I have
Distant signs unfurl emotions in me
this sunset won't be my last
Sunsets are my meditation
time I take for self
Moments of isolated celebration
give praises if nothing else
Quiet introspection witness to
the subtle rhythms of the Earth
Peaceful time for reflection
chance to script a little verse
Poems to thank the Creator
this moment is my church
Space for reconciliation
as I reflect upon my search
Simply breathing & being
I ponder on my fate
Wonder what my words will sing
what lesson they might relate
What insights might I receive
if I let my mind just wander
What secrets thoughts will tell
given time to ponder

Another beautiful transition
citrine day cascading night
I listen to my inner being
creator of what I write
Unwaveringly I stare
hawkeye sun gold center

41

Watching fall skies threaten rain
and oncoming chill of winter
I query my spirit
what is it that I must do
What are my new dreams goals
where is fate leading to
Will I counsel I know I'll write
I guess its back to school
I'm off to Mercer to study poetry
I guess that's kind of cool
Then to graduate studies
maybe get a Master's degree
Who knows after that
I'll just have to go & see
People with disabilities
need confident voices to lead the way
& I guess its part my fate
or at least that's what I think they say
Warm Springs for the winter
options cottage developing lifetime skills
Writing reading drawing
catching sunsets before my meals

The New Dawn

I know the feeling
of pity as people look down
but I also know in my heart
about things yet to come around
Kryon 11:11 Baktun 13
cryptic words though their unsure
I know what they mean

I'll play out this role
let fate prescribe as is allowed
just a part of my supreme lesson
fulfill my Sacred vows
What is one lifetime
in the immortal journey of soul
just a scene of happening
in the longest movie to unfold

We'll laugh about the unfolding together
as performance ends
Joke about the lives we've had
roles we've passed as friends
others too are here to spread word
having heard hint about the way
seers of the new dawn
reinterpreting signs of coming day

One life sharing insights
relate experiences that we've had
try to awaken those still sleeping
who happen upon our path

Cycling here and about
thrown from one lesson to another
memories forgotten secrets coming out
there's more yet to discover

Where I am
there I am
together and alone
Consciously blessed in knowing
feeling close to home

So what can I say not already said
I am more than just a seeker
that found the Grateful Dead
I was home before all that
though still upon a search
Looking for others knowing also
there role upon this Earth
There are more awakening
hungry for simple clue
A time ago there weren't many
but now there's quite a few

Dusting Off The Savior

Those that lent careful ear
never realized full extent of scribing story
for them later in coming

They knew Spirit loved him
signs were many imbuing revelation

They never believed though
it would lead to this

Spit on coerced stoned in detestation
he waded through hostile streets
a man hated for Truth

None knew
so many would aspire his murder
or that the pain would be so great

Can he help he was chosen

Words of mock disdain
spread to cross in criminal offering
nails hammered plunged spike
through the soft meat of wrist and bone
crushing ankles staking arms outstretched

Displayed like ornament
arms spread in hugging gesture
head dripping blood
from gash of crowning thorns

Splintered he was raised for all to view

Few here loved him as she
most teasing him of foolish crusade
scolding him as the King of Jews
offering for the conquest of Rome

Hastening his demise
a soldier guard jabbed his side
hardened spear shaft
gutting him in shocked squeal

Shriek arose with parting soul
As Yashuah exclaimed
'Father to thee I commend my spirit'

The sky blackened sun
eclipsed by moon swallowing
the universe of stars appeared as testimony
crying out sparing no tear
for the severity of the moment

Christ the savior is fallen

Disability Nights
by Gabriella

Zen, your poems swept through me, cleaned me,
shook me, sprinkled me out
like dust on the open carpet --

Did you choose your last name (Garcia)
for your
hero (Jerry)?
sweet-thinking, slow
blinking, how you
been walking that road

I loved your handwriting
ought to frame it
knowing the tears
behind each shiver
the art within --

I know about effort
though I live a different layer
I'm lying here in
bed writing this,
squashed by gravity --
I managed to grab
a pen and diary
got to get it down
trapped by pillows and paralysis
tears and temper --

Well back in the old
days, we might have
drummed together --
swam naked - climbed a hill
and laughed 'till the sun set

Instead, we're meeting in a
different vein
though I see clearly
the ore in the crystal
and how deep it runs.

We'll be friends forever man --
and let your pen speak it out
Don't hold back - you're there
shout it out however loud --

I want to give you a
gift back
like you give life
and I see you've given
one to me --

Seeing you gives me a glimpse
of what I give others --
Snailing along in this chair
Sailing along --
Singing my song --
Singing my song.

Blessings to you
Zen
and thanks

Enchanted Evening
for Gabriella
in response to Disability Nights

Outside musing
beneath cotton puff clouds
Apollo sun warns of Spring
fresh hairs of green
sprouting wings
from pregnant Earth

Freedom once again
3 bedroom
3 miles from Mercer
$300 a month
for 2 years or more

Kind sister to assist
96 Ford Windstar as chariot
new growth abounds in a world
mysterious with changes

Almost through with 'Evening'
scanning the final rendition now
my orchestra muse
she sings always
so much even
that sometimes I must ignore

My life experience
the inspiration of my words
shaping me shocking to have found them
& myself in this strange
applaud able moment

I know sweet sister
the disillusion
of your space
thoughts your mind perceives

Disability is different yes
but always remember
blessed are we
to grace Creation
with the eye
of our conscious soul
& I know you know
your words tell me so
you are one like me

Morning flowers sunrise
it is the promise I anticipate in wait
the chill of remembering
knowing tears flowing undenied

Observing all things observing
part of all that is was & will ever be

Reverence for my life
the essence of my being
the evanescence of this moment now
every dream I've ever seen

You're right soul sister
we meet in different light
posting the strangest roles
we've ever known
but who better to help those
swept beneath the rug

Somersaulting Tomorrows
by Gabriella
in response to Enchanted Evening

Brother, your letter came at a good time.
But any time with you is good.
For your words are in a pool not of time
but of pearly connection
to an unseen now.

You said, "remember
blessed are we to grace Creation
with the eye
of our conscious soul"

Your words turn me somersaulting
into a sure tomorrow
where dreams and reality do not clash
with uncertain heat or cold nights,
flip me backwards into a yesterday
childhood innocence cats-to-pet
oceans to wade, mud-between-toes,
brothers-to-tease, strawberries-to-pick,
room-to-clean, homework-to-do
How could we know?
Why didn't we see?

And these words throw me out of yesteryear
and tomorrow's fear
into that pool of the ocean's glow
Ocean of love –
that dissolves my pyramids of time
blossoms and swallows them
into Herself for safe keeping.

So now our poems can dance together
as once
we would have mulberried-round-the bush
or farmer-in-the-delled.
or treehouse-built or dolphin-swam.

You say, "who better to help
those swept
beneath the rug?"
I love the way you waste not a word,
how can you afford to?
I am lush and overstuffed
with my metaphors

But then that is the dance
of yin and yang.

Ping-pong with me!

-G

Natural Mystic

Splatter of constellations
the Old Ones watch us laughing
chasing our tails in all seriousness
running to stand still

Able America eyes scan over
they assume lives better
because of jobs lending identity
evading center wrapped up in chasing illusion

The Earth grand in variety
spirals a tight ellipse around a fantasy of light
tonight that itself revolves
around some great center

Missing point they consider not
harmony of forces driving it to this
I await the coming
scripting thoughts
exploring the visions
of some voice inside

Doubts spark adventure
signs of progress restore lost faith

Smiling on faces
fearful of my stare
ignorant of what I bring
I look for seekers everywhere
closer than they think

All roads lead home

New Love

We dance
butterfly angels
strewn to wind soft dreams
she tentative at first
unsure how to be
I would wait to catch her eye
with tenderousity
now she straightens my feet
without break in conversation

She's the kind of girl
having met
I could wish to meet again
soft spoken
laughing in quiet smiles

Closet expectations
for me
to wither a broken man
the disabled plight
fight for basic rights
& dignity
we are what we wish to be
not what others think they see

& she knows like me
it will take more
than quiet frustration
to make the change
civil disobedience
if necessary

'No Pity' for callous minds
citing laws insensitive
to the people's needs
we've come this far
lead follow
or get the hell out of the way

Me
I'm erecting a new altar
in honor of difference
and she likes the attention
of being with me
great parking good seats
we cut lines most of the time
& people
some really go out of their way
to display
the lost kindness of humanity

On sunny days
she'll cat into my lap
easing my chair back
we'll dream away high
mellow in comfort

Perfect for quick spring naps
& star-packed nights
nothing quite like
her head on my shoulder
sweet smelling hair curling my cheek

Love was different
but never better

The Matrix

Programmed from the ages of 0-18
we are informed by public education and agenda
to study for comprehensive tests
that insure our correct incorporation into
what the system claims as reality

It's around 15 that we start to question
the relevance authenticity of social belief

Public education is wholly predisposed
and it's widely known
most people in country are not even included
in what has been handed down
as the official history

Modern America is acculturated
into educational philosophies
which uphold only the opinions
of those who conquered through history
whose interpretations
no longer hold real meaning
for what is now life relevance

They the contingent only want us to conform
be the good slave little worker bee
tamed by visions of hellfire damnation
self denying guilt blame and shame

I left all that crap behind
went seeking freedom outside world approval
receiving lesson from land
creatures Spirits I'd met

Outside the mad insanity of cultural beliefs
I didn't care if no one else could see
what to me was insane measure

I could not would not live up
to a life pleasing others expectation

How long do they think
it can go on like this

Enough of the bullshit
time to throw the vagrants from the temple
replace the system
and leaders guiding it to this

Chapter 3 – The Beautiful People

-Tom Olin

Now is the time of your deciding. Now is the hour of choice. You have come – as has your species – to a crossroads. You will select, in the days and weeks, months and years immediately ahead, how you want life to be on your planet – or if you want life to be on your planet at all.

This is my message to the world: You *can* create a new kind of civilization. You *can* seek a newer world. The option is yours. The moment is at hand. This is your moment of grace. Use this moment. *Seize the day.* And begin by choosing, in this moment of grace, to become more than you have ever been or dreamed of being; to reach beyond your own reach; to remember that nothing is beyond reach.

See yourself as the light that will truly light the world. Declare yourself to be so. Announce it to your heart, and then, *through* your heart, to everyone. Let your actions be your announcement. Fill your world with love.

Know that you are the savior for whom all have waited, come to save everyone whose life you touch from any thought they may ever have that would deny the wonder of who they are, and the glory of their eternal communion with God.

-Neale Donald Walsch

The Beautiful People
ADAPT 1996 Atlanta

Praise the Most High
I have found others
united in voice
passioned in struggle
attentive ear cast
to the suffering cries
of brothers and sisters
thrown away dying
in cruel institutions

Rally up International Boulevard
to Olympic Centennial Park
where the bombing occurred
terrorizing peace time games

We were an awesome spectacle
of long slanking weave
single row of wheelchairs
snaking to horizon view

Loud mantric chants cries for justice
a serpent of energy crawling
scaled in florescent signs
inked in logos promoting
rage for order
myself carrying one
scratched in big black
permanent marker
"Pissed Off
And Ready To Get Shit Done"
flashing it to all who care to look

Poised in
strange tense like anxiety
excitement anger enflamed
for common sense theme

Give people back their lives
options opportunities right to life
freedom of choice

We knew things were screwed
in whatever way we came to know
what mattered now is that we knew
and because we knew
we were going to do something about it

II. Frank and Victor

My first action
ADAPT was amazing
the brotherhood sisterhood fellowship
of all peoples gathered

I was overwhelmed that so many
came from so far
so dedicated
willing to risk health
and arrest if necessary

One story burned to mind
I knew would interpret poem
a man blind to sight
& perceptual expressions
knowing others by voice alone
was the assistant hands
and means to action
of another man larger
paralyzed from neck down

Trading hand for eyes
rooted in brotherhood
one pushes
one voices
together
they make their path through history

III. Gathering Of The Tribes

Strategic effort insight
plotted the merging of forces
such as these

Like Lord Of The Rings
ADAPT united in voice
came together to clever change

Newt Gingrich was scared
having heard ADAPT was in town
he decided on
meeting with delegates
before more focus
was shed his way
trying to prevent possibly
siege of his regional offices
or home in Marietta
memories of Michigan haunting his mind

A few from the leadership posse
met with him and came back with words
we've heard before

Decision was then made to lay asunder
Congressional Headquarters
Democratic National Convention

This would be a week
of staying up all night
of waiting for buses
to take us to jail

Overwhelmed by sheer numbers
and complications
officers didn't know what to do
dreading the paperwork
as 86 ended up being arrested

Clinton sensing riot
sent quick response
and Presidential aide
to assess situation

Word came from Air Force 1
that the president promised to look into
ADAPT's bill
the Community Attendant Services Act
and long term care choice

Wide media coverage
locked his words
to history

In the morning the welcome arrival
of sunrise and caravan of vans
awaiting release from jail
ride back to hotel
emerging to loud applause
and shouts of praise

Civil rights warriors
returned from battle
needing food sleep and dreams
to do it all again

IV. Aftermath

Mid-afternoon traffic
everyone trying to get home
from jobs and habit day

Imagine a major multi-lane highway
shutdown completely
among wild cries of dissent
4 lanes of freeway goers blockaded
by a line of wheelchair users
handcuffed in unison

Unable to budge an inch
or do a thing about it
wayfarers were extremely pissed
having their secure little lives disrupted
by a forced change in routine

This evening when all of America
would tune in to see
who would serve them as President
into the new millennium
they would find ADAPT ruling headlines

The world looks on in bewilderment
spying scene from helicopter view
Eagle eye a dark sea of writhing lights
wheelchairs strapped
people bound linked in cuffs
crossing wide median
intermingled in effort
desperate attempt to voice frustration
bring focus to cause

How far do they want us to go
people are dying
every 3 minutes alone
in some hide-away
piss smelling nursing home

120 were locked up
in the take-over
of Memorial Drive
500+ in wheelchairs
swarming with friends
cameras flashing video rolling
3 hours before Presidential election polls
were to close

The Nazis pre-holocaust Europe
used propaganda films
to justify genocide
proving it economically sound
to exterminate people with disabilities
calling it 'Existence Without Life'

At least they offered
a quick gaseous death
as opposed to a lifetime
of hopeless stagnation

V. The Marriot Marquis

Night action decided
we were off to the Marquis
hosting convention for HCFA
the healthcare finance administration
confront the organizers responsible
for nursing home death and opinion

Overwhelming defiance
there would be no subtlety
to this act of civil disobedience

Patrons looked on in shocking disbelief
as ADAPT members
flung themselves from their chairs
every 3 minutes
in remembrance and honor
to the forgotten soldiers
of the forgotten war
those alone dying in nursing home
one of us under the flag
of disability

120 more were arrested challenging the system
and its callous ways
among swift political gesture loud yells of protest
people exited top-floor rooms
to see what was up

These people are more real
more alive
than many full bodied souls
stagnating in routine

My first national action
it would not be my last

I love these people
ADAPT is so ripe in passion
and every bit as fun
as any group I'd been around
each unique in way tendency
doing things as we do
in cool peculiar style

I see the rest of America
complaining about this or that
complaining but not doing jack
anger spilling empty words

America can learn from ADAPT
needs ADAPT to get things done

What we do is for everyone
cause mission justified righteous

Like the Deadheads
I have new family
a feeling of coming home
like being found all over again
true to my colors

What The Hell Are You Staring At

Staring eyes everywhere I go
take a fricken photo

Noticed not for tie-dye or long hair
but wheelchair
standing out like an armored tank
on a freeway of cars

People gape at me
over the naked green-haired guy
pissing in the corner
with Prince Albert
and 12 inch dick

Did I piss on myself
stream puddle
out the back of my chair

Do I have crap on my face
a humongous zit
whitehead poking through
pressure awaiting release

What can I do
to satisfy your curiosity

Why the looks
like I escaped from the zoo
or have been profiled
on America's Most Wanted

Pugilist Response

TV proliferates the attention
of so called civilized society
on subtle campaigns for tobacco
and unhealthy foods
while the leading cause of deaths
are emphysema lung cancer and obesity

They also pervert social focus
with an unhealthy bombardment
of sex murder and violence

Hollywood blockbusters sell
the newest hot model
willing to expose skin
while blending storyline
with the newest most exotic way to kill
or blow something up

We honor serial killers on Biography
like heroes of insane worlds
describing in grim detail
their laborious attempts
of plotting gruesome murder

CNN and daily news keep everyone up with
the new madness molesting streets
of our nation and world

Glorifying war terror global conflict
police arrest and gangster crime
The Sopranos are the new "hit" series
for all to see

Our children become desensitized
to all the insanity
entertaining themselves
with video games promoting callous death
killing in video excitement

Gladiator culture
we love Jerry Springer
and pugilist response to conflict resolution
attack at commencing bell

What's the message here?

Everyone's asking
what's wrong with the kids
what's wrong with us

They say I'm just a crazy punk kid
talking about stupid things
I say we're a bunch of blind idiots
living a stupid dream
They ask me why don't I wake up
and join everyone in reality
I said what the hell do you know of reality

Slaving the Grind

Kids wives hard lives
never-ending commitments
new mouths to feed

Endless tasks of work
money to assure monthly payment
stave off ever amassing bills & credit debt

Shackled to vocation
servant to corporation
intervening thoughts of what if I just left
said screw it all

Where would one go
what would one do
so much to consider
how does one contend
mounting frustration

Many are simply losing it
pissed off in their own worlds
angry at one thing or another
miserable to the point
of stepping off deep end

Pledged allegiance
oath to industry
sharing 15 minute cigarette breaks
with others
comfortable in complaining
joking about changing it all

Many work 60 hours a week
just trying to break even
living off habit toxins
responsible to insane commitments
picked up along the way

Sometimes their only reprieve
besides sleep and dreams
is that long heated ritual morning shower
with power enough
to soothe away cruel feeling
drain away smug oblivion
cease to exist
if only for moments
nozzle rain heaven in faucet delivery

Faulty Appraisal

I think of my son
wonder about his doing
what preoccupation intrigues his fantasy

I think of his mother
protracted memories
of first love gone wrong

Sometimes children
are the ghosts of those earlier dreams
reminder of lost times
haunting impression of broken relating
when whatever something fails
and trust is evaporated

Parents and children parted
many families
are strung along on loose connections
a web of mangled occasion
and lost opportunity

There are fathers like myself
everyday having children
unready even to determine their own lives
much less the fate of some other

The Angel Sun

The burgundy fall sun rises late
and is quick to settle
days shorter
night grows increasingly long

Deprived of light
winds get colder
animal coats thicken
harvesting winter food

Construction breaks
workers flee to kids wives
hungry for quick meals
& favorite shows

Skeleton trees
stand naked bare
dressed in auburn shades
eclipsing the quiet here
between cars of people going home
ascertaining beauty
in stolen glimpses
from windows along winding roads

II. A 1000 Fairies Dance Upon The Lake

Clouds rushing come to go
forcing crisp once fluorescent leaves
into puddles upon the ground

The angel sun erupts
from amidst the clouds
a thousand fairies dance upon the lake

Hawkeye God sun vision green
blinded as witness
I burn this moment's presence to mind
wind howling scattering pages
of Solara's 11:11

Apricot and fading
the Sun glimmers final retreat
center of our foreseeable universe
light and life giving orb
departing horizon
yielding to night
sprinkle of dreams
world moving to shade

III. Night and Her Purple Legion

Crescent moon mid height
to my left shoulder
twilight another world awakens

Chilly the wind whispers softly
in silent retreat
rippling a ghost mirror lake

Temperatures recede a billion leaves
scatter roadside ditches

An abandoned light pole salutes day lost
from where it stands
emerged in shallow water

Waiting for ancient and docile stars
fighting off the cold
I remember nights like this
we spent exploring curious yearnings
on plush green grass
lying in soft cotton puff blankets
tight for heat

Velvet Night riddle of stars
splattered constellations decorate skies
divided by legend and astrology

Never did we mind the cold
we would always chance night
to wrap up in the glory of young love

Darkness settling twilight almost over
crickets harp sweet chirps
serenading chorus night

We pleasured nights just like this
burning each other for love
answering questions of one another
happily lost together

Found in each other
the wind more present
cold more defined
my neck stiffens calling for warmth
see you manana Angel Sun
we'll do it all again

Ode for Winifred Jones - 38
Friend and Victim of Nursing Home Death

O great death final calling
I am ready for your parting embrace
release me from this ill suited fate
where I have found myself bound and confined

Have they no compassion
no consideration for what they do
locking me away as if I've committed graven crime

I am just a man in longing of company
someone to confide in
who might understand
to care about me

We shall cross again in stranger space
bent on delivering different story

But alas it is done
tremor to me your finger frozen in time
relentless in pursuing
swift me away to different dream reaper
I am tired and in need
of new circumstance

Claim this body used and battered
scarred by years and memories
of time when freedom was disposition

Salvation rests
in the angels parting wings
music of homecoming

Chapter 4 – Can't Find My Way Home

-Tom Olin

Religion has separated man from God, man from man, man from woman-some religions actually telling man that he is above woman, even as it claims God is above man-thus setting the stage for the greatest travesties ever foisted upon half the human race.

I tell you this: God is not above man, and man is not above woman-that is not the "natural order of things"-but it is the way everyone who had power (namely, men) wished it was when they formed their male-worship religions, systematically editing out half the material from their final version of the "holy scriptures" and twisting the rest to fit the mold of their male model of the world.

It is religion which insists to this very day that women are somehow less, somehow second-class spiritual citizens, somehow not "suited" to teach the Word of God, preach the Word of God, or minister to the people.

Like children, you are still arguing, over which gender is ordained by Me to be My priests! I tell you this: you are all priests. Every single one of you. There is no one person or class of people more "suited" to do My work than any other. But so many of you are just like your nations. Power hungry. They do not like to share power, merely exercise it. Yet I tell you this: God's greatest gift is sharing of God's power.

I would have you be like Me.

–Neale Donald Walsch

Kings Owning All Pleasure

They'll try at all cost
to make you guilty for all you do

Sin they say is original condition
and all that feels good wrong

I don't care about their definition
they have no experience
no truth to placate assessment
of mystery

All they have are words
not even their own

Let them figure it out
in meantime I'll live as a king
owning all pleasure

Artistic Endeavor

She would hold me when she could
focus distracted I had my art
my words

Self contained
she couldn't understand
life was all I needed

I shared what I could
it wasn't enough
and I knew

It's always that way
my coming and going
muse lead

Steady whispers taunt of freedom
and me
I am always readily persuaded

I hope she is nowhere suffering tears
beating herself up over
what may have gone wrong

Some are appeased only
by the blackest silence of night
solitude of artistic endeavor

Beg of No Tomorrow

Love me today
if you wish
or abscond for another

I promise you
only this moment
no treasures I have in store

Gauche as it seems
no erection lasts forever

Shannanda Moonspiral

The
fly ass
hippy
chick
with unsettling
eyes and carefree
demeanor
didn't notice
me at first
and I
didn't care
I drank
of her beauty
anyways
savoring
it for
later
in
spir
ation
*

Voice Of Inspiration

Quell the voice of inspiration
what do you mean
you want to be an artist-
you're going to school
to be a doctor or lawyer
earn money to pay your own bills

So says the contingent proclaiming wage
the most important task
of life accomplishment

Must develop skill worthy of profit
food drink clothing jewelry
car house spouse
everything depends on success
and success depends on how much money
one look like one had

Most neither rich nor good looking
credit cards allow one to extend charade
expand capacity for moments of celebration
in smoke filled bars
with others drinking wage hard earned
also hoping for respite in another's company

I did it different doing what I loved
without regard to money

Poems were my resolve
allowing me to seduce meaning
into awkward situations
fill time with thoughtful undertaking

Why chance encounter
when one could plot conquest
she was mine
if I could extract the right words
and I knew

Years passed
without debt I have my freedom
watching others like dream
come and go

Some would never realize
until too late

I write now for me alone
must give heed
to that voice inside
that feeling no other can fulfill

Cathedral Grove

Red moon glow
words soft remedy
for occasion

She seeks me for rendezvous
among stone carved relic
walking hallowed ground
in keen soft step

Crosses huge ornate
decorate space in lost garden appeal

I watch her
unannounced for pleasure
if only to see
the slow century
of her grace unfolding

Justin

My son now 6
me in miniature form
worlds different
we are the same

If I would have stayed
to watch him grow
how different would he be
Would I know the things I know
would I see the things I see

He sits in my lap
driving my electric chair
impervious
to glancing eyes

Setting up his army men
he hands me the dice
to throw and knock them down
instead I roll
he loses six men

Monopoly monster
he plays all sides
but of course he always wins

He doesn't understand
the implications of my injury
or think me broken at all
I still beat him at Nintendo
& he likes the way I draw

He says you walk
Let me ride

A model now
paid to decorate pages
He'll fly to a New York
to pose for school boy ads

Summer in the big city
freedom for his mom
He'll wonder one day
about words woven
into the tapestry of my poems
articles I've so patiently written

He prays at night
before fading to dreams
wishing I could walk
so he can have
my electric chair

One day he'll reach a point
where he will challenge
the dreams & pointless goals
of children more lost than he

From my great grandfather to me
they will go to him
& make him wonder

Wondering he will come to me
with questions
he does not yet remember

I'll be here to explain
the passions of my soul
things that go unknown
for they will be unable
to answer or understand
his special difference

Not All Are Forsaken

Night elongates
asking me to its quiet
I am a breath away and waiting

She does not notice me
in still posture
quietly undone

I see her nervousness
fear of being swallowed
by shadows and darkness

I yell my voice beacons her way
some hear me some don't
I gesture when inclined

She reached me with kiss
stars riddling night
not all are lost in orbit

Thoughts Upon Waking

The wild innocence sprung from your eyes
was just enough to mesmerize
those who dare to look
a chance I took though I understood
things were not great but were looking good
and you thought I was kidding
with the look that I gave
but I told you in gesture all I needed to say

Her hair shutters soft wind
eyes darkest brown
She moves like a phantom whisper
slow gesture little sound
Soliloquy wind lullaby
full moon on the rise
Words never spoken
revealed in smiling eyes
Wafting mountain breeze
glazing lengths of silky hair
As gentle as her feather voice
parting the winter air
Wide expanding clouds recede
as another sunset dies away
I'm sure that I can satisfy
her mood in every way

Lake Vista, Warner Robbins, Georgia

Early morning silence ripped
by phantom jets on occasional flight
how sumptuous life is
in those raw wilderness moments
of concentrated thought

Cats cradle my dormant legs
Fluffy Thumper Cheyenne
puddle against one another
Brenda arrives
they attack feet begging new meal

7:30 begin done by 9
stretches range of motion
long heated shower
followed by ritual massage

Senior year early classical poetry class
last quarter 1999 at Mercer U

I exit my apartment
cross the street to the pier
morning rushing
sun climbing still
clouds loosely gathered
gawky geese fly in large V fellowship
honking to announce arrival

Families of mallards and white ducks
shake and dunk morning baths
with tennis ball children
dressed in fresh feathers

All harmonious quiet
children leaving
parents having gone to work

This is my church
world my altar
words my prayer
opportunity to say
thank you Great Spirit
for even these moments now

Sway

Did you see her
the girl with the swallow hair
feathered back in breezy lengths

She had that creamy walk
that just begged you for display

Visually stunning
I would pass her by anytime
for the one authentic in thought
and deeper relating

All my life I have escorted strange vixens
to carnality and pleasure
hoping one day to meet the one
who would understand
the mad ravings of my tongue

Wonder if that was her?

Not Dead Yet

Among you for short time
settled in this curious role
Machavellic performance
Shakespearean style

Watch me pass this life
in grand theatrics
touching every diamond star twinkling
celestial night sky

Life weird beyond words
scenes I enter now
political forums
a room of pressed suits
television cameras
people of persuasion
able to impact laws
unjustly set

I want change
more than that I want justice
I see need in the suffered eye
of ravaged souls once
myself needing aid

Service dharma
I want to help
brothers & sisters
who like me
were once shattered
beyond description
who now face unbelievable circumstance

Utmost compassion
I wish them strength
in their time of need
because I know
their unbelievable pain
the space they experience now

And if I can work
to ease their struggle
even for single moment
then I will fight
for opportunity
to bring light to their lives

Remembrance of my own shadowing
mother wailing tears
father choking them back
trying to be strong but obviously crushed
unable to gaze into my eyes
hollow and withdrawn

Nervous desperation
death trying to steal me away

Their only child
I river tears now
& it feels good
because those days are gone
& I made it through

Now I must help
as we all must help
for the time that I am here

I must do something
to ease someone's pain
& make sure
no one has to go through
the hell I went through
to get to where I am

Praise the Spirit
that brought me this far

Think For Yourself Tour
Winter 1997 DC

Colors stagnate withered
by brisk ghetto wind
crisp late October cool
as morning shades stiff in retreating

Burned-out winter sun
late rising
grants little heat leaving world
in artic still

Neck taut
500 hundred gathered
from myriad directions
to form single unit
and make this dream happen
guided by leaders honed in skill
years of protest
and hundreds of civil actions

It is important that we
inform you of our wishes
ensure focus upon cause worthy of investigation

If need be
we will risk jail
health illness injury
death even to achieve
freedom for ourselves
and countless others who have no choice
no right to even know
that others care they are suffering

Politics won't do anything
until we push them to proceed
it's not their life at stake yet

It's taken years of work
to get MiCASA this far
so many heroes lost
but not forgotten

Certainly some sort of change
will soon yet prevail
this ADAPT guarantees

II. Bust on Bilirakis

Target Bilirakis
head of the environmental/health subcommittee
where MiCASA stagnates stifled in paperwork
awaiting consideration
stumped by congressional nonchalance
bureaucratic red-tape
and lobbyist pay-off

Our friends are dying
as they claim budget lack
when wasting more money
than the cost of freedom

We want a date for introduction
promise of action now
we told you our homes
or your offices
& we meant it

Break past security
swift invasion forcing opportunity
we charged in streaming down
Rayburn passenger corridors
smiling at the people wondering
what was going on

We were in before they knew what was up
& by then it was way late

It's silly the way they try to hold out
making bullshit promises like this
is some amateur organization

Like we'll just leave
we posted siege
laying up hallway space
for 5 hours through 5 drafts of promises
until demands were sufficiently met
giving media time to cop their story

They'd never seen anything like it
immune hidden away from it all
in a DC building on a DC street
protected by distance & current legislation

ADAPT will never willingly allow our country
to perpetuate nursing home bias
and domestic holocaust

So we came massive in proportions
blitzkrieg style
to effect change
and make it known
institutional bias has not will not
nor ever could serve the freewill
of the people

III. Concluding Requiem

Fierce in confidence
willing to do what it takes
we gave strong presence
while still allowing free access
to labyrinth passages
so they could draft their proposals
& do our work

We were creating lasting memory
sharing older war stories
with newer soldiers
embedding impression
imprinting lives momentarily touched
but permanently tattooed

They'll never forget us
or what we did here today
having learned and sided with our cause

Finally in written terms
letterhead reply
-MiCASA would go before subcommittee
March first quarter of 98

We had our date
mission accomplished
we filtered out
ecstatic over accomplishment
knowing we were heading
in right direction

IV. Shakedown at the CBO

Next point of attack
the Congressional Budget Office
overseers of National fundage
& first step of a bill's chance of approval

Always sneak attack
special forces style
20 penetrated far corridors
of endless halls

Chancing intervention
they took Oneill's office
the rest of us held mass protest
throughout the rest of the building
handcuffing chairs to location
blocking elevators entrances exits

"We're ADAPT your trapped get used to it"

"Just like a nursing home you can't get out"

Sounds of justice now the waiting begins
sheer numbers effect legislation
when nothing else can

The CBO says it's to expensive
to pass MiCASA
that it has no plausible chance
anytime in near future
of becoming a real bill

Well that's unacceptable
and we want resolution
demand it or we don't leave

Give us signed promise
to look it over again
with us in house
to assure quality focus

Want to know what we need ask us

Hours passed until they
emerged from cubbyhole offices
with words to appease our passion
like Billirakis they would meet
with members of the leadership posse
to reassess current points of view

Letterhead proclamation
a tall bush headed women
with strong resonating voice
announced their defeat
with official declaration

Cheers resonated throughout the building
shouts of triumph
claps of joy spread news of victory
ending in meeting the following Wednesday

In & Out smooth flowing
clockwork style
"The people united
will never be defeated!"

No blood spilled soldiers lost
no families to suffer

We went home with that feeling
of doing undeniable good
for those forgotten and unspoken for

Streaming out
heading home for post feast strategy
night was for celebration
T-shirt sales friends and laughter
time to hang out
converse over a few beers
before drowning in sleep
night metamorphosis
healing to do it all again

Chapter 5 – Forever Moments

- Tom Olin

Classes in critical thinking, problem solving, and logic are considered by many parents threatening. They want such classes out of the curriculum. As well they might, if they want to protect their way of life. Because children who are allowed to develop their own critical thinking processes are very much likely to *abandon* their parents' morals, standards, and entire way of life. In order to protect your way of life, you have built an education system based upon the development in the child of memories, not abilities. Children are taught to *remember* facts and fictions-the fictions each society has set up about itself-rather than given the ability to discover and create their own truths.

Programs calling for children to develop *abilities* and *skills* rather than *memories* are soundly ridiculed by those who imagine that they know what a child needs to learn. Yet what you have been teaching your children has led your world *toward* ignorance, not away from it. Schools serve their students when they share with Young Ones what Elders have learned and discovered, decided and chosen in the past. In your schools, however, you present these data to the student as That Which Is Right, when the data really should be offered as simply that; data. Past Data should not be the basis of Present Truth. Data from prior time or experience should always and only be the basis for new questions. Always the treasure should be in the question, not in the answer.

-Neale Donald Walsch

The Concrete Jungle

The Angel Sun warns of Spring
fresh hairs of growth
returning birds
early blossom to gardens
in dire need of flowering blossoms

Eager for reentry into college
dreams of school
they asked "What religion are you?"

I said "All of them."
laughing inside
at the puzzlement
on their faces

She asked me what happened out there-

I said I've seen it different

I've stayed among people
who run naked all day
work or play
& celebrate nights
in a sweat lodge
by the moon sautéed River

I've seen the Angel sun
deep rim the wide Pacific
dead red crash & burn horizon view

I watched Yellowstone River fall
from towering heights
sacrificing itself into a spectrum
of rainbow hues dashing & smoothing
ancient moss caked rocks
in wait far below

I've lived in Jackson Hole
where the Snake River
scissors past the dormant pose
of Sleeping Indian
portrait carved mountain cliffs
sharp wind raw reserves
hailed as national treasure

I've done ceremony
where the Redwoods stand old & glorious
dwarfing ancient forests
steamy in spider morning dew

I've dug quartz crystals
from Mount Ida in Arkansas
where the land is thickly laden with fine veins
of scattered points
everywhere clusters so giving of themselves

I've been to the northern rim
looked out over the edge of a deep canyon abyss
where labyrinth mountains
wall in a slithering sliver
of ribbon river still cutting away
deep terraces puzzled over jigsaw chasms

They'll never know
what they had to give
for education

Book angled views
opinions formed from words
other than their own

Where are the new prophets
to forecast the next legacy of this tale

Find out then compare
words with others
sharing their own

In youthful innocence
we conquered mountains
climbing the highest trees

Immortal we pushed
into frontiers anew
eager for the unfound fruits of life

Now words & film define our lives
being all we see
losing ourselves in false worlds
reality can this be

Praise the Most High
that I know different & better

I'll play this role
pass this dream smiling
praising all reward

For Zeyla Now 7 Months Broken

Raven night alone with laptop
Fiona whispers 'Sullen Girl'

Traffic slow in passing
I stare into screen mesmerized
romancing thoughts of Zeyla
7 months broken

Spider scaling a mountain wall
supports failed and
she plummeted 30 feet
smashing her back at T-7

I met her
at Lakewood Amphitheatre
during the Rage/Wu-Tang Show
southeast of ATL

Weeks earlier she had written to me
appealing empathy
having seen me on the cover
of Spinal Column magazine

I wrote her back
with words of encouragement
sending her 'When The Evening Dies'
for persuasive inspiration

Kindred occasion brought us together
hair thin black & flowing
20 years old and beautiful

Zeyla wheels beside me
in subtle Quickie grace
measuring her strokes
with still awkward precision

I watch her entertained
by the new inspiration
she brings my life

Chilling time spring days together
she would transfer into my lap
tilting my chair back
we would share kisses and conversation

Wherever we go
we roll with confidence
turning heads with no thought of concern

Funny the looks people send
inescapable attention wheelchair appeal
they will look
without doubt some will stare

She is learning
ignoring the smirks
settling into space and situation
getting used to the idea of always being
center attraction

Time will teach her to adjust
find serenity in her still new awkward situation

Me I'm here enjoying the ride
regardless what they say

Columbine

The contingent would have us believe
it's the best it's ever been
that our economy is getting stronger
and the market indices will rise forever
increasing wage

It doesn't matter that the children
flower in ghetto violence
taxed by drugs and disease
toting pistols for privilege and revenge

I weep with the young ones
still not registering effect
ghosts of bullet punctured lives
parents confused in candor
for children lost
stolen from world

Ask the Columbine mothers
families enduring loss
peers whose friends were killed
by incomprehensible callous crime
if things are just peachy

They'll tell you different

Boxed Paradise

They live side by side
in $350,000 homes
built on 1/2 acre lots
with neighbors on all sides

Witness to each other's
successful extravagance
competing credit debt
alarms keep accumulated property secure
while dogs guard perimeter against intrusion

Asphalt streets allow easy patrol
of gated communities
locked in secure proximity

Vagabond
I applaud your freedom
to own only what you can hold
and just go

The Contingent

Our child rearing ways are dangerous
and it has been proven amongst our teens

"Bowling For Columbine"
is an interesting synopsis
of current societal condition
cultural fascination with guns
and mounting murder rate

We can no longer pacify child curiosity
with Playstation and violent TV

Our network outpouring
is breeding little soldiers
who have no conscious sanctity for life

The Native Americans watched children in play
saw how natural inclination leads interest
then encouraged curiosity to future occupation

We nurture children
with odd TV programming
depictions of violence and horrific murder
calling it entertainment for the masses

If we are to learn to embrace peace
with each other and ourselves
peace is what must be seen known felt
glorified by what we see everyday
depicted by movies network and news crews

Stories of good will
service to one another
caring empathy for family friends creatures
inhabitants' elements of Earth
and Earth herself

We can achieve what we so willfully desire
why not desire peace

The system proposes
slave only to be normal
never question authority
or challenge the way things are

1 percent are leaders
you are not part of those elite
just succumb to set policy
cattle through life following direction

It was set up this way for you
to save you the trouble
of having to think on it too hard

They say - trust us
you'll love the way it is
all of this is for you
because we love you
and want you to work hard
so you can enjoy some of what we have later
when you're old enough
and worn out enough to retire

Internet World

Never have we as a world culture
had access to the same information
and in identical universal way

Computers have erased
the prejudice of difference
surpassing boundaries borders
bringing accumulated knowledge
safeguarded tribal wisdom
to all people
granting access to all worlds
no matter skin color race gender or disability

From any corner anywhere
any individual understanding
the rituals of the Net
can log on to its grand transformational experience
and make it their own

All situations can be explored
all knowledge art music media sought out
and introspected in ways
unthinkable until now

One can assume anonymity
absolve bodily identity enter space secretly
connect to chance encounter circumstance
with others in similar pursuit

One world intricately bound
we are onepeople@Earth.com

Silk Embrace

Last days light cracking worlds
windy breeze blown day fading darkness
stubborn stars appear
to cast night in new mystery

We sat intrigued utterly bewildered
awestruck by the magnitude of beauty
available in a moments prestige

Radiant Venus
diamond light beautiful watching
my involvement in world

Some of my friends are locked away
incarcerated by misfortune/institutional setting
surveying Wheel of Fortune
over minimal substance dinners
and 12 ounce cans of Coke

I am lucky to be on the out
kissing the girl with carnival eyes
copulating words and interest
giving to what beckons
moments of summer love

No television could ever grant
the charity of her silk embrace

They deserve this
this all that I am

Moonflower

I never offered you word of this
when you were here
jewelling my horizon

Aftershock of spinal cord injury
severe pain mixed with non-feeling

Gathering what was left of the unbroken
I didn't understand your incorporation
into my life at that time

Foolish I asserted to not allow sympathy
to enflame your passion
pity I prescribed must not be excuse

Responding in shambles clouded indifference
await the right one they say
dressed in deja-vu smile
and coincidental sign

I chose to let you escape
wanting to watch you fly
rather than bar your freedom

By the time I realized good fortune
fate had prescribed you to another
who were we to upset
challenge then

It was only later that I fancied your smile
time we spent amusing our presence together

The last time I spoke with you
you said you missed my slap happy ass
laughter we shared
in response to situation

You were different with me
we both knew
and though I didn't relieve your eyes
of what they had hoped
that was then these words for now
and though you may never see them
at least I feel better

Significance of Babel

Separation still curses our intent
do you not remember
the detail of those years
past lives bringing it to this

History fails in mention
what soul has seen

With but narrative
I could smite your confusion
clothe you in knowing
unveil the pretense parading as reality

Comprehension available only to them ready
you'd never believe me though
how far-out legends reveal

Reason fails to enrapture
not my job to convert
hint only
to those having set sail
mark direction for them
seeking passage beyond
to often bizarre realm

Most are afraid of unknown depths
skirting shores
thinking world flat

I'm with the island girls
in celebration of new religion

Nobody led me
or said this way
I sailed alone on makeshift raft
with wind as companion
fate for deliverance
confidence enough to assess
new disposition

Do not forget
the myth of our coming
soon we will praise heroes
of stranger tales
than even my own

This Way to Paradise

Watch where it is you wander friend
the dark night has strange requiem

Mythic acclaim promises new season
for those blessed to interpret meaning

Recognition dawns the eye
never any coincidental meeting

Come I await you
this way to paradise

Reluctant Father

Nothing can ever reclaim
memories forever lost in passing
distant from recollection

No amount of words
no matter how earnest
can ever restore actions left undone
words left unsaid

I was too young to understand
the beautiful miracle initiating birth
of wet new soul
return to awkward world view

Selfish leisure lead me
to decision I felt correct at time
in moments that I made them

Only later did certain regret set in
realizing the consequence of past decision
I was left in futile mood vacant
with uncharacteristic need to be fulfilled

Thank God Stacy was so strong
in her fervor to make it
caring for you with odds hugely
stacked against her

Poems I've written
during the course of my wandering
compare nothing to her kind mothering
and parenting example

I won't try to justify distance
circumstances leading it to this
or claim further declarations
on what was what might have been

I write this now to somehow ease situation
ask you with so many people in your life
who care for you worry about you
wish the best for you

Do you need me
feel hollowness like me
want to know what I do
what I am about
and where you come from

Do you want me to be
a part of who you are
and will be in future relating

You will soon be a man
separating self defining individuality

I haven't been there
for one reason or another
to guide your struggle
give answer to questions you may have

I'm so willing if you will allow me
if your family will allow me
to help and assist you
in any pursuit interest you may have

Perhaps one day soon we may share
meal and conversation
amuse strange avenues
life has imparted

In you is the future
of my every tomorrow
the blessing and answers
our world so desperately needs

Son you are the answer to questions
the universe has yet to ask
and it is
just a matter of time
until you unveil your genius

Enchanted Twilight

Rapturous morning movement born again
butterflies flay clumsily toward
the parade of ghost cars
darting by in rapid fashion

Wuuusssssshhh penetrating
sheet-rock walls to thin to dim
I'm in bed now
squashed by laptop & paralysis
deciding poem
chasing elusive thought
until it leaves me defeated
with only sunrise
as comfort for opinion

Life cycles I watch it's unfolding
plotting goals and dreams
blessed with a Waiver
that allows me freedom to choose
spatial unfolding

It will be warm & beautiful today
the calm will break
gathering populace for breakfast
the freeways will crawl with steel
people head for work & school
dogwoods unfolding secret petals
to sunny rays
another moment of blessed assembly

The Last Rose Of Summer

I glanced her coming
specter nonchalant along my path
ghost moonlight silhouette of faded trees

Fazing my world with her chill intrigue
she said her name was Karena
'she who brings the rain with gentle wind'

I am here she said to reinterpret
the multitude of signs
for them going further

To me she offered her gifts
unquestioning I gladly received them

Years ago and still shaken
a seraph from all I could tell
her salutation
my welcomed reception of paradise

Displaced by encounter
gone with morning star and inkling dream
no trace of her being near

I was left with that disconcerting feeling
that something was amiss
to previous pondering

Never again witness
to the frailty of her touch
the arc of her waist
gemstone eyes or ocean smile

My voice never conferred
the scope of this lexis
carefully lain to page
in her honor

Hazy on the details
all I know is we were alone
with nothing but black night
checkered stars
and moonlit intention

The smell of her gathered
leading me through
idle wind
and threat of morning

Chapter 6 – We Shall Overcome

- Tom Olin

- Tom Olin

I saw an ancient path, an ancient road, traveled by the Rightly Self-awakened Ones of former times. And what is that ancient path, that ancient road, traveled by the Rightly Self-awakened Ones of former times?

Just this noble eightfold path: right view, right resolve, right speech, right action, right livelihood, right effort, right mindfulness, right concentration... I followed that path. Following it, I came to direct knowledge of birth... becoming... clinging... craving... feeling... contact... the six sense media... name-&-form... consciousness, direct knowledge of the origination of consciousness, direct knowledge of the cessation of consciousness, direct knowledge of the path leading to the cessation of consciousness. I followed that path.

"Following it, I came to direct knowledge of fabrications, direct knowledge of the origination of fabrications, direct knowledge of the cessation of fabrications, direct knowledge of the path leading to the cessation of fabrications. Knowing that directly, I have revealed it to monks, nuns, male lay followers & female lay followers, so that this holy life has become powerful, rich, detailed, well-populated, wide-spread, proclaimed among celestial & human beings."

-The Buddha
Samyutta Nikaya XII.65 Nagara Sutta

Forced Meditation

Life with disability
strange endeavor
interesting its lessons of patience
and meditation

The wounded martyr
prostrates rare form
challenging soul to understanding
far greater than normal routine

We wear all masks sooner or later

Whatever hurricaned my inception
into strange fate initially
is gone forever part of past
untouchable to me now

I can only live here as fully
and as functionally
as ability allows

Four years ago today
my life changed
and all I thought I was
became a dream
and all I am now possibility

Crown of the Babylon

DC my second action
first where I really played a role
as color leader
feeling proud of being part
of something that truly mattered

They can't really expect us
to allow what's going on to continue
as they sit in cabinet assemblies
making decisions on what's best
for "those people"

They think our minds impaired
because of different ways of being

They fail to realize "those people"
are they one day with injury or age
they are we

Reclaiming power
we force notice
into areas of our lives
which we best understand

Our goal: CASA
(Community Attendant Services Act)
rally public political support awareness
promised action on topic
of nursing home bias

Stop selling our lives
to big money institutions
lobbying laws unhealthy and cruel

ADAPT our power to change
target sites secretly then charge forward
capture and lay siege
until demands are met or arrest draws near

Media attention always important to cause
it gets nasty at times
keeping it together while police swarm
and angers enflame

We manage well enough
protesting with structured objective
sharing more than just words
to make difference

I myself
am proud to be disabled
dislabeled claiming
unity with my brothers and sisters
fierce in protest
willing beyond arrest
to defy for denied rights

Challenge brings results
the Monday after returning to Atlanta
from our sabbatical in DC
I got word C.A.S.A. had been introduced
as House Bill 2020

Star Streak

2 a.m. meteor showers
firmament ablaze
atmosphere igniting comet debris
flaming heaven in boreal streaks

Bitter freezing cold
harsh November wind
near a vacant lake
stiff night silent in retreat
all we needed was a warm fire
to persuade our stay

I watched huddling Tra' and blanket
as Amanda and Shannon
gathered pine straw
small branch for fuel

Love is thrilling in commencement
9 years her elder
giving self to me

Our attraction gradually unfolding
assigning circumstance
to fresher benefit

She knew we would be lovers
I knew
it was merely a matter of time

Vagabond Scribe

Years ago life was pacing highway
in 86 Ford Aerostar van
sleeping on a tri-fold out foam mattress
unnoticed near chain hotels hostels
near Grand National Parks

Freedom then was an atlas the road
money enough to make it
meals cooked on a Coleman stove
Arizona flavored iced teas
and bottled water for beverage

No commitments dates hurries
places necessary to agenda
no particular everyday contact
disruption or distraction

No cell phone or beeper
I was drifting wandering with moment
seeking cool experience to drama memory

Bare necessity a backpack tent sleeping bag
snowboard skateboard mountain bike
books notebook and few changes of clothes

Everyone should chance to leave at least once
allow self time to pursue willingness to wander

Every moment fresh
each moment alive and free
I found answers I found her
enveloped beautifully in mystery

Suburban Centaur

Disability has tied me to the city
and its tendencies

The non-stop stream of noise
steady pound
of always something going on

Though I used to live
outside the scope
of political policy and disorganization
breaking my neck has left me
to the mercy of their legislation
and what they do in office

Their callous disregard of others
affects me directly
I am bound
like most everyone else to insane measures
dictating corporate biases

Trapped in worlds ruled by network TV
sex sells product
environment secondary to economic prosperity

The masses don't even realize situation
how ecosystems are because of cities
tuning nights to selective viewing
worshipping idol shows
and cultural programming

We know only what they tell us
truth a well propagated lie

Propaganda creates belief
I want to leave it all
run wild naked free
hang with the island girls
smoking cloves
on beaches of powdered sand
sun cascading view
nature gripping me
in strange persuasion

Somewhere the sun rises
and sets on water
ocean courted by summer rays
shimmers in moon night

Sobriety

Restless high school tedium
lead to trouble for me
breaking probation I ended up
in a treatment facility for 59 days
a month after turning 17

They said I must learn
to mold with society
stop rebelling against systems
dictating our lives

Required AA/NA meetings
recovering addicts spoke of peace sobriety
in between chain smoking
long drags of dark cloud
and gulps of coffee black as night

Overcoming addiction they said
is awareness of the issue

Y2K

Shuddered by uncanny feeling
thoughts of a new millennium approaching fast

Jupiter moon fading landscape intrigue
will we survive the next 100 years
slaughtering habitat
laying concrete garden
so no one must maintain the grass

December and still spring warm outside
they say there's nothing to the greenhouse effect
jet emissions clouding sky in exhaust fume

All around me life is linked
to meaningless endeavor

Y2K on the horizon
computer bug possibility of corrupting
entire control systems
and maintenance technologies

Who knows what will happen next

Multi-million dollar research studies
proclaim no scientific proof
that desecrating the rainforests
dumping toxic wastes into oceans
and damming every once free-flowing river
will have or has
any lasting effect on environment

Do they really think us that stupid

Earth first in all things
something will have to happen
to hold us if but for moments in our tracks
give world time to reflect on situation
shatter opinion of what we think
we know as reality defined

Force us to take notice
of what we're doing as a species
in regard to the bigger picture

Maybe the Hopi will have the last laugh
poke fun of our loose dependence
on cruel technologies

The future may not be as secure as assumed
maybe soon existing systems will fail
procuring necessary change

100 years ago horse's carried distance
now shuttles push limits of sky
capable of escaping the Earth's gravity

No matter how many bulletin boards are erected
wires strung or concrete laid
no place would I rather be

Sometimes we do more harm than good
this we must apprehend
weighing benefit with concern
of children and future regard

Star Child

Word soft remedy for occasion
son I want you to know
I've been dreaming about you
and your mother

I pray all is well
that you are taken care of
and loved in the way a child should be

I hope this letter
finds you in good health
claiming daily pleasure from everyday living

I have written many times
without hearing from you
rambled on about things
that you are maybe still to young to fully grasp

So many years have passed
without me sending word
at times I thought it best
if I just remained in the shadows
not interfere with the daily routine
of your current family affair

I don't feel I deserve the right to know
all of what's going on with you
though I wonder frequently

Finishing my 3rd and 4th book simultaneously
I hope that I will be able to one day soon
share with you the work I have done

I hope one day
you will be able to see me perform
in fencing tournaments
poetry readings here and abroad

I wish I knew what involved
your focused attention
what drove your passions and will for fun

I dream of conversation with you
meaningful dialogue
time in which we can set aside difference
past behavior embracing moments anew

Labor through the chaos
which separates us even now

I love you son with tenderness
I never knew before

Fate is driving the force
to bring us together
this I believe
soon our worlds will collide
and we will be left facing each other
with new incident to celebrate

New Dawn Morning Rising

The Dragon Lady rose
hungry to prophesy

Left in parting kiss
stiff paralysis
fresh memories of her waking

Gone before the others came
our tryst a secret

She helped me process day
dress bathe get into wheelchair
in between love
idle moment and comfort thought

Waiting for Brenda
to begin morning routine
sometimes life is so great
candy delicious

Night is for her soft lips
and careful metaphor

Beautiful Freak

Don't judge me
friend brother sister
there is only One
honored above all
worthy of that deed

New morning sunrise
through thick shaded trees
summer back deck
lizard lounging

Distant mower blaring throttle high
distraught dogs bark
pent-up in square cornered yards
of square cornered lots
of urban blocked America

Babylon existence
daily suburban life
mellow in mind
8:30 early morning
traffic steady pouring noise
outside the hollow walls
of our roadside crib

Behind the shriek of urban life
the still soft hummingbird hum
subtle peace
eerie morning shadow song
of cricket cicadas
doing their thing

Families of birds
hatchlings sound rooftop heights
announcing presence
praising the life giving orb
rising in steady progress

Helios in ascent
spreading thin ringed
rose gold fingers to Dawn
white robed in glittering glory

Night recedes
sunrise on the lips of morning

Terrestrial sanctuary
ceremonial fanning of light
to the Tall Ones
holding arms always upright
high in constant prayer

Stretching always for golden warmth
green leafed fingers expand
budding blossoms
like thorn roses erect on steady stem

Their firm lives spent seeking out distant heat
reaching for source
like kamikaze moths imposing flame
suicidal in desire
effort to get back to the Light

4 days of appeasing rainbow rains
lifeblood for the chain of children
linked so delicately to one another

I've missed you
Bright One
your smile on my face
warmth of your grace
distinguishable from all others

Sky magnificence
Angel Sun
bright-winged
so giving of pleasure

I salute you saluting me
home in the midst of it all
I play to complete no return trip

Christ knew Tarot-like
he was to die
at betraying hands
prophecy for martyr blood

What is one life in immortal journey of soul
a window of a moment
just a fragment of the whole

Confident Living

Dislabled
I am capable
of more than they assume

What will they do when illusion is shattered
disrupting all world's fray

Life differently rewarding
these wheels are my freedom
tool to challenge accessibility

Fencing writing reading drawing
semi-retired I spend my days
doing whatever I want

Raphael replied when asked to serve the King
'Should I make myself more prosperous
by a road I find repulsive?
and yet now I live just as I wish-
a blessing which I suspect comes
to very few men in high position.'

I need not money to manage affairs
I trust I can always handle situation
find the right person willing to assist
pass chill time with kind Athenian sisters
scripting words for their leisure
a fool musing harem

Blessed with these moments now
responsible for aiding those seeking way
I do what is prescribed by light and new agenda

Silence Most Never Contend

Recreation
re-creation of that which you are
I am what I am
to know thine self
is to know the great mystery

Silence most never contend
afraid to be alone
in wilderness home
where strange phenomena occur

Yashuah fasted in wilderness preparation
eager to meet the desert spirits
who would come to test his claim

Usurping the temptations of three trials
he returned to culture
a man now prophet and messiah

A little faded before I ever
sat in wheelchair
doing things different
from prescribed routine

I wanted to know what was up
why we were headed
the way we were

Why things considered education
made no sense at all
people not doing as they say
or saying as they do

I did those things important to self knowing
okay with sticking out
like a sore thumb
pimple among the masses

This chair is not who I am
though an integral part of me
I am what most cannot hope to see
okay with self
even if people laugh
because they misunderstand

Disability was my wake-up call
no more skirting shores
waiting for rain to settle

Time to set bearing for deep ocean
into the eye of the hurricane
no tomorrow to wait

Centered in the midst of it all
I know where
the paper-wing butterflies
gather in abundance
and sunsets are always free to see

Laid Up

Shadows push evening
wind rattling trees
all I want to do is
get out in the sun
burnish skin in warm calm

I'd do anything to stop throbbing
sitting increasing pain
forced discomfort
I'm drifting light headed fuzzy
clobbered by ache
hydrocodones masking intensity

Will I ever feel better
why can't they tell me what's wrong

This feeling has to be more
than just sitting
others seem less affected
less crumpled by posture

I know something's wrong
breathing hurts
my body jumping from stabbing jolts

7 emergency room visits later
and still no correct diagnosis or remedy
how can I endure forcing tenure

More pain pills
resolve to eat so I don't puke
cortisone shots help existence a few days longer

I can't imagine what I would feel
if I weren't paralyzed
supposedly disconnected
from feeling capacity

Try explaining to doctors feeling
when they assume you don't

Loaded light floaty
feeling ill insomnia sleep affected
melatonin and temazapan
to help me sleep through the pain

Working poems for 'A Different Way Of Being'
shifting head and foot adjustments
bed seconding as my office
access to water computer
paper book and pen

Rest is healing salvation
maybe tomorrow
the sun will come out
and I'll feel better

Chapter 7 – Enduring Tragedy

-Tom Olin

Dream of a world in which love is the answer to every question, the response to every situation, the experience in every moment.

Dream of a world in which Life, and that which supports Life, is the highest value, receives the highest honor, and has its highest expression.

Dream of a world in which freedom becomes the highest expression of Life, in which no one who claims to love another seeks to restrict another, and in which all are allowed to express the glory of their being in measure full and true.

Dream of a world in which equal opportunity is granted to all, equal resources are available to all, and equal dignity is accorded to all, so that all may experience equally the unequaled wonder of Life.

Dream of a world in which judgment is never again visited by one upon another, in which conditions are never again laid down before love is offered, and in which fear is never again seen as a means of respect.

Dream of a world in which differences do not produce divisions, individual expression does not produce separation and the greatness of The Whole is reflected in the greatness of its parts.

Dream of a world in which suffering is never again ignored, in which intolerance is never again expressed, and in which hatred is never again experienced by anyone.

-Neale Donald Walsch

Pink

I've come to love you
more than words
can effort to say

I want you this moment
your honey lips
somewhere seeking
catalyst to inspire
poems in your own way

How I see myself
defined in your gentle form
young visionary random scribe
filling world with story
prophet of next day's lesson

I watch her contend phrase
preserving moment
a Taurus
lover of moon and song
stars as parading company

I am ruled by sun
a Leo
alone with poem
shadow wind trailing
distant prophecy

Muse Of Broken Wing

Young one suffering haste
I wish her more than anything
effortless well-being
better when she lays on me
and expects me to love her

Time easy in passing
tranquil as saving grace
she sleeps eyes gelled
Celtic dragon tattoo adorning shoulder
perky breasts
nipples pierced by silver balled ring

Chill moments of winter
together late night
her lips parted in breathe
head comfortable pressure against my shoulder
knee draped across my waist

Lost in her splendor moments
I love her
dawn finds me feeding her touch
with my own

No better refuge than this bed
given to her distraction
stranded with muse of broken wing

Wheeler Dude

Quiet respect keeps some distant
compassion intriguing others
to engage conversation

I offer my attention
eye contact inviting dialogue
impact slicing through judgment
and preconceived notion

I ease their attraction with smile
testing curiosity

Many will look
no doubt some will stare

It doesn't bother me
what they think
worlds they imagine for mine

I am defined by my own creation
situation belonging to me alone

Surrounded by the kindest friends
empathically sensuous sisters
those who work for me
so willing to assist
be part of my world

I'm blessed to not be barred in institution
where people strand others
in a moment of crisis
or if the check no longer comes through

Stiff in seclusion
restless with only TV as company
I see their bodies ate up by sores
lying in filth
waiting for someone
anyone to enter earshot
willing to shift positioning

Where would I be
without the waiver
home with senior parents
wearing them thin
pushing them to their own demise

I give so much praise
gratitude to the many
that have assisted me
to get this far
each in own peculiarity

Thank you for allowing me
time to experience memories
entwined with your life and living

Thanks for chance
to present even these words now

Deja-Vu Disability

I turned 17 at a juvenile treatment facility
called Turning Point
near Moultrie, Georgia

Before I left
I met a guy named Mike
new to the adolescent program

We didn't know each other
and never got time to really hang-out
I was leaving to face the real world
a still confused teen
trying to change friends
ways of being lifestyle and routine

I got heavily involved with martial arts
girl named Stacy

A year later Turning Point called
asked if I would visit Mike
at the Shepherd Spinal Center
in downtown Atlanta

They said he'd broke his neck
diving into a shallow lake
somewhere in South Georgia

At the time I knew nothing really
of what exactly paralysis
or 'breaking your neck' really meant

The next day Stacy and I visited him laid up
hidden away in hospital sheets
and multitude of blankets
pink cushioned foam collar stabilizing neck

He had a metal framed halo
attached to his head
stiffening cervical alignment
wearisome family surrounding
trying to comfort situation
crying to handle concern

I'm not sure he recognized me at all
machines blinking toning life support
private second floor room
single window view

We stayed with him for while
his family left us alone grateful for the break
giving us time to re-establish connection

I told him I was sorry
that he'd get better
soon things would refer back to normal

I never realized I lied
and that he's probably in wheelchair even now

I had all but forgotten him
until I recalled the whole scene
arriving by ambulance jet
from a sunny beautifully warm California
where I had spent the past years of life
establishing self

To what seemed the same room
of the same floor
of the same hospital
I had visited 6 years prior

Recalling incidents
amazing how idle moments elicit memory

In Shepherd myself
with probably the same injury
trying to figure fated meaning
over restless persuasion

I am still learning reasons why
content with situation
doing life a little differently
but loving it all the more

Evolving Relations

Beautiful relating much struggle
bringing it to this

Parents are children too
pretending to be responsible
in mature attitude

Just as lost
we act out in defiance purging self
processing evolution
growing through tears & laughter
gathering memories
lessons in daily passing

Families define love
sometimes in crazy interpretation
even with good intention especially young

Children watch in confusion
the conflict of parental relating
screams manic moments
anger enflamed words let lose
statements to wound or kill
miscuing crimes of passion
never meaning to hurt deeply

Children learn about relationship
patterns whether healthy or insane
from witnessing parental behaviors

They/We mimic these cycles
in our own struggles

Learning to treat others
from what we were witness to see

In evolving
we establish what we want to hold on to
and what we must discard
when tired of painful routines
redefining patterns of unrequited love
we so willfully desire

I've watched my parents evolve
30 years of marriage
and can honestly say
I could only hope
to find one such as my mother
and be the husband my father exampled to me

I give thanks to them
for their beautiful relating
and privilege of being their son

Daily Word August 19, 1997

27 today years fading
like sprinkled stars in dawn's horizon
arrival of sun threatening new day

Life ever blessed
new unfolding intercedes classroom convening

I am older wiser
relaxed in my paralysis breathing with it
learning the patience it demands

My friend Dominic and I are entertaining
idea for provider agency
doing all I can to help self and others
stay out of pain
learning from my body as I go

With ADAPT over 2 years now
disturbed by disability history
the horrors of accepted treatment
millions locked away confined to die

I'm glad to have met others
also disgruntled by
the nonchalant attitudes of some
who think things are alright the way they are

In every face I see myself
it could be me living in nursing home
abandoned by life
discarded like a broken doll
trashed by once proud owner

Doing what I can
to help in long term care policy
giving opinion to boards and task force

The Waiver saved me
saves me even as friends strangers
are left contending refuge
in dire straits

Things will change
ADAPT will change them
doing what we need to foster
a new era of civil rights
for a community of people
still denied fair access to life and living

Lead
follow
or get the hell out of the way

For Gaia

Remember once when we used to pass
celebrate spring and harvest
cloaked in white
trailing candles
through wine dark morning

Chant dance and pray
ritual among ancient stones
temples aligned to equinox
stars in proper alignment

Forgive us for forgetting
of our need for you
Earth mother

Christmas Charity

Evening dies
panther night withdrawing
the bright promise
of glowing stars
& luminous constellation dreams

Morning eclipse broken
Christmas dawn rises
beaconing clouds
vaulting heaven in shock color

Mars Sun
blood red morning
embracing wide backed sky
in puff of pearlescent haze

I sit amazed
humbled by the trembled hues
interceding procession
night giving way to morning

6 years paralyzed
hip hassled
by all day sitting
still thankful for being
not all are given chance
to resume breathing

Christmas no holiday for the trees
I think of those less fortunate
starving unsheltered with no hope
of what to do

I want to give to them
please others
if only for moments

Spark a tinge of hope for those
who have nothing
nothing to give
expecting nothing
not even phone call

Saint of Circumstance

Life's most relevant teachers
exampled service to humanity
and each other

The greatest duty
giving without expectation
needing nothing in return
living without regard
of learned prejudice

Humble moments
filled with gratitude
grateful for any choice to action

Wise intent always in occasion
loved for righteous illustration
humanity idolizes saintly figures
placing them on pedestals
said unreachable to common man
who then never appeals to try

Declared saint
deeper meaning aligns the action
of servants
eloping strange reward

We are they
they are we

Namaste O Mitakye Asin
forever yours
I will to will thy will

Enduring Tragedy

Relationship post injury
bound my family
like no time prior

We were disjointed in the past
seeking separate endeavor
entertaining life habits alone

My routine was work/school
martial arts sparring
weights late night
stretches in sauna/steam room

Injury prepared us remember
imbuing life with deeper meaning
dissolving petty difference
meaningless to essential relating

New perspective brought new values
ways of communing
I'm a better person now
having learned from near dying
battling now for the rights of myself
and others

Discrimination forces one to rise up
if your disabled you're labeled
and must own up to the fight

ADAPT provided me a means
to channel anger fueled
as I learned about disability history

Others cared what was up
and that made all difference
for cause greater than my own

Working the political front
trenching protest 60's style
2000 a new millennium
and we're still denied
fair access to freedom

Proving there's yet more to do
God just know you're forgiven
and thanks for the parents life
no money can buy

For Them That Might Understand

Suzanne and I read poems
a full two hours
to motley gentle crowd
ready for my dish

Back-room scene
bean-bag posh
soft oriental intimacy
as they gathered before me cradling space
upon color matted floor

Back-room back-door
downtown Golden Bough book store
CJ fingering soft keys
setting tone
for quiet introspection

Mellow mood séance enchanted
fragrant incense to spice air
no cooler group one could call
to assembly

Wind chimes gentle music
calm pace
soft words setting space
generating relaxation

Tonight I would give them pieces of my life
they would see beyond
the mask of my fate as I reopen
forgotten wounds
joyous memory

Treasured moments sculpted
forming fragmentary poetry
vision of paradise lost
and found

Sharp slice of knife
thick throbbing vein
free wet crimson blood
words dripping slowly
precious life
the offering of poetic soul

Opening Midsummer's Night
followed by Natural Mystic
Suzanne with Concrete Jungle
then collaboration
on Inspired Soul

20 or so other poems trailing reflection
selections covering the past 4 years
of my life's strange coursing

Lacing thought in deep confessional voice
how everyone hung amazed
on every syllable word
breathing as I breathe
pausing as I pause
to look up into their faces

Suzanne theatrically inclined
how swift and sure-footed she was
bounding sentence in gymnastic grace
tumbling word to word
fueling imagination

175

The poems faded one by one
with black-mooned Night
creeping westward under blanket of darkness
drapery of stars trailing

I felt we succeeded
if only for moments
to jester in space
opening them to contemplation
riddled my own way
occasion fading
with words hinting verbal decree

.

So Many Roads

Young and misconstrued
relegated to wander
my path diverged from yours

No excuse to suggest
I was determining self
trying to know rather than believe

No reviving past opportunity
I look on to future with new wisdom
achieved from days that lie between

All history set aside
can you accept my resignation
forgive me new intrusion
grant me chance to know you again

Together
we'll push new boundaries
in ways they never conceived we could

Love you son
I wonder about your days
ways you play
and what you do

Time will settle all mystery
bring new event to facilitate
new memory

Hope to see you soon

177

Chapter 8 – Endeavor Freedom

-Melinda Beasley

-Tom Olin

Deception is part of government, for few people would choose to be governed the way they are-few would choose to be governed at all- unless government convinced them that its decisions were for their own good. This is a hard convincing, for most people plainly see the foolishness in government. So government must lie to at least try to hold the people's loyalty.

Government is the perfect portrayer of the accuracy of the axiom that if you lie big enough, long enough, the lie becomes the "truth." People in power must never let the public know how they came to power-nor all that they've done and are willing to do to stay there.

Truth and politics do not and cannot mix because politics is the art of saying only what needs to be said-and saying it in just the right way-in order to achieve a desired end. Not all politics are bad, but the art of politics is a practical art. It recognizes with great candor the psychology of most people. It simply notices that most people operate out of self-interest. So politics is the way that people of power seek to convince you that their self-interest is your own.

Originally, governments had very limited functions. Their purpose was simply to "preserve and protect." Then someone added "provide." When governments began to be the people's provider as well as the people's protector, governments started creating society, rather than preserving it.

-Neale Donald Walsch

St. Louis, Missouri
National Governors Association
ADAPT Rage For Order Tour 1999

15 hour Greyhound trek
endured in laughter
fewer of us this time
being regional action
it would be easier
for police to contend

With Clinton in route to speech
the National Governors Association
heightened security was impending

The air electric tension bubbled
as they barred us
from the Adams Mark Hotel
where all 50 Governors stayed

Inside eating cheesecake and sipping wine
most governors unanimously believe
disabled lives unworthy
of quality of life accommodation
pledging support to Olmstead
and States rights to place people
into institutional care
while at the same time fining them
for cruel and unusual punishment

Many are dying
waiting their whole lives
hoping something would change
needing someone to care

Advocacy is life for many of us
must make it easier for others
everyday cannot be a struggle
someday resolution
must assume strange displacement

Jesse (The Body) Ventura
independent party governor of Minnesota
and infamous wrestling renown
trespassed police lines
to meet us
and address our concerns

It was the only direct acknowledgment
from any of our 50 elected officials
and as we left from protesting the first day
city workers with police escort
extended barricades
2 city blocks in every direction

Unable to access their convention
the leadership posse
conspired assault on buses ordained
for the evening event

Having trouble locating carriage
Mike and Greg spent
an hour and a half
hunting up and down
the streets of St. Louis
looking for their buses
as everyone else
awaited appointed destination

It was then "The Bus God" delivered
14 shiny white NGA stagecoach buses
right out in front of
our Regal Riverfront hotel

Spotting them
Bob Kafka returned in frenzy
rallying troops to ascend on positions
blockading every bus if we could

With promise of an exquisite
four stars Steak Dinner
for the first to capture bus
everyone accelerated for door

In less than 2 minutes
35 ADAPT members were handcuffed
body and chair
to a fleet of buses idling quietly
waiting to gather Governors company

Heather, Freedom, Dremmel, and I
took front line
on the 2nd row of NGA buses
electing to pass being behind carriers
swamped in exhaust fumes

Some drivers were irate
obviously disturbed
by our presence
honking horns
one giving us the finger

Soon madness lined streets
photographers' news crews
state and city police swarmed
among dancing lights and flashing cams

Every station showed up
in matter of minutes
to gather what would be headline news

We gave them our story
told them of institutional bias
lives being lost

ADAPT can not simply allow
decimation policy
to control fate and fortune
of a huge population of people
who choose choice
and want alternatives in healthcare placement

We uphold the conscious right
of all beings everywhere
to equal access
and fair participation
in inclusive environments
promoting health and well-being

It is not right for corporations to profit
at the expense of people

Our country was founded on
civil disobedience
rebellion against oppressive tyranny
contriving declaration for independence

We shall not rest until vindicated
35 were arrested 33 of us went to jail
as 5 hours passed while we were processed
gathered fingerprinted and detained

None minded fighting for the equal rights
of all people
jail was just another day
advocating for those locked away
dying in cruel institutions

Dinner was a bologna sandwich
which I gave away
sandwich bag of Fritos 2 oatmeal cookies
an orange and some water-downed juice

19 wheelers and one able body
locked up in the same cell
those who could assisted those who needed help

Genuine scene of grand brotherhood
women in a different cell
sang songs of freedom

"We shall overcome
we shall overcome someday
deep in my heart I do believe
we shall overcome someday."

We spent the evening relaying stories
getting to know each other better
over conversations of previous arrests
shared laughter
and oranges peeled by a stranger's hand

Masters of Creation

The insects animals trees of natural wonder
live in peaceful disregard
to our wise civilized ways

Science would have us believe
that Nature has no soul
and that we are the only conscious entities
in the entire universe

That statement in itself
denotes ignorance
the Everything watches the great importance
we assume our lives entail

Waiting for us to awaken
from superior separation

How wise are we
that we can't even care for our own home

185

Glance on Time

Unfathomable sophistication
the life giving drama
cycle of rain sun seasons
transfusing hydro-energy
flushing land
enabling abounding life & sound

Myself forever found now
speak words in time
leaving thought meant unspoken
for them latter to define

Claiming to know
only what I've seen & felt
in the deep adventure of exploring soul

Doubting all you throw before me
no mindless brute
look about see which creature
walks in weird angles
lost among it all

Silent creeping wide-eyed
& steady breathing
I am a serpent
among tall grass

Renewed Beginning

I opted to chase road to adventure
and self discovery
thinking about you as you'd grow

I did what I felt right for the time
seeking answers
questions
questions to answers

I carried you with me
in heart
crossing roads and sunset horizons

Wondering often of your progress
and what significance was spurring growth

So pleased to have heard from you
I am thankful
so very pleased
life has brought us full circle
to unite story

Praise God Stacy found a man
worthy of her embrace
unoccupied by worry
mature enough to handle
love she has to offer

The one thing I felt unresolved
the one hole emptying soul
the one decision haunting my life destiny
has finally been concluded

Our now ritual chats
and checking in
sharing what was held back all those years
has filled me
fulfilled me for rest of journey

I found answers I needed out there
trailing fragment truths
piecing together puzzles
reconstructing delusions hampering man

All my found secrets
every poem anecdote
is for you Justin
all I do for you

You are my greatest legacy
my greatest joy
I'm proud of you
and delighted to have you back in circle

Praise everything leading it to this

Grand Casino Hotel

Its 11:30 now my parents sleep
nestling dreams with deep breathing

I've been writing since 7:12
allowing thought to flow pages
which will someday portray moment's occasion

At any time I can sit with silence
open myself to poems that come

It's not always been this easy
I've been writing now 18 years

I know not every thing I scribe
will be relevant for passing
some memories must remain untouched by word

Some occasions needn't conspire
phrased parable or thoughtful undertaking
I write to fulfill need
give heed to that voice inside that says
"Listen, I have things to say."

I'll never know if it's the same
for others
most care not to listen

Self-proclaimed prophet
of new millennium
I dictate songs to interest
leaving hint to them
who may later need

Fade to Black

I am fading my back hurts
arms tired fighting off sleep
though I'm flowing so well

I want one more poem to mark occasion
give rise to voice inside

Praise the Most High
for conscience being
night to the Spirit of musing
the Dragon Lady at home
awaiting our next engaging discourse

The ocean churns quietly
lulling night in peaceful lullaby
I must flip onto my stomach
lessen the pain of posture
give my back the reprieve it will need
to acquaint day in new rendering

Good night sweet muse
of uncertain word
let us dance again tomorrow
in new poem

Momentary Zen

Words read right for those
whose experience matches meaning

I wonder what they see
and if it's beyond this wheelchair

I can't allow their interpretation
to rule my world

Each person defines self
in what limitations
we ourselves infect upon life

Freedom is self defining
being okay with who you are
where you are
for the time
pleasure of being there
here

Morning Sanctuary

Some wander to and fro evading center
courting internal dialogue
as it distracts focus
with material entertainment
to fulfill moment
day to day

Forced into meditation
disability has made me extremely aware
awake with dream

Trying to positively vibe world
share light along way
in harmony
aligned to the rhythms of the giant family

The Mayan ancestors try to imbue
through ritual and calendar
sacredness in all moments
ceremony in all being

Church is living everyday ritual
waking eating drinking sleeping dreaming
'I am' is a moment of prayer

Stumbling through stillness
paralysis and pain
seeking life's warm calm

I am making the best
of all I am
and can be

S.A.D. - Social Anxiety Disorder

She is gone
and I am alone
thank God
salvation is my own

So perfect
our relationship now smitten
she faded
the dark corridor
of dank hallway
eyes darting in avoidance
mood absorbed
in sad countenance

Mean demeanor
why do you hate world girl
warped in paranoid thought
cold to audience

Forgive me retreat
nothing can be rightly said
I do not understand
it seems foreign to me
the strangeness of your predicament
and why everything
bugs you so

So bothered by all you can't control
how can life be
so difficult
when I pamper you
providing for your every need

Does every dawn
bring more trouble your way
do you not see
feel the sunshine of day
life so beautiful
burnishing soft skin
in warm chastity

I don't know what to do
to help you
but maybe if you feel better
I'll hold you tomorrow

Carrion

I loved you
until I couldn't spare the pieces
to satisfy your vixen ways

Incredible while it lasted
no denying
I still dream of your moments of kindness
hungering for your relief
soothing quake of your touch
love focused my way

Maybe I wouldn't have been marooned this way
if we had just ended it sooner

We didn't and here I am
still thinking we could have saved each other
when no one else could

You would have dragged me down
fed off my carcass
until there was fresh meat to devour

I couldn't let it happen
not needing more psychodrama
on top of what I was already trying to handle

I wish you well in your every endeavor
beautiful child
maybe we can share journey
later in the trip

Irreconcilable Differences

She sought to own me
even knowing what I must do

I couldn't help
she needed so much more
than I professed to give

Too far too fast
can we recompense time shared
redeeming those definitions
prior to love's ugly form

I wanted what was paramount for us both
succeeded only in
escalating your madness

Can you own the river flowing free
pushing wind to measure
escorting ocean awaiting progress

Paradise Kingdom

Aware always
where I am in moment
trying not to mix energy
with those creating misery
through insane conduct
attracting karma consequence

Learning to recognize cycles patterns
wisdom of higher teaching
I am rambling free
one now to next

No particular affiliation or set way
knowing of the teachings
of Jesus Buddha Krishna Mohammed
and the others

One must find Spirit
in personal awakening
give thanks to Creator Creation
in ones own way

Magnificent Earth
temple worthy of housing the holy
praise the Most High
for my conscience being
may I act on what I know

Visual Inspiration
- For Tracy Simpson

When she enters room
every head turns to see
she is like diamond moon
waves as caressing company

You can hear them rumor
trying to chance a casual stare
conversation humor
long looks from those who dare

Every direction boys and men
fixate their glancing eyes
trying to contend her beauty swiftly
chance the press of her passing guise

Reason of life for many
American dream kids wife family
all their lives they have waited patient
hoping to catch a jewel such as she

Visually inspiriting Tracy
conjures every head spin and turn
slinking like a runway model
she makes every beating heart yearn

They wish to comfort her embrace
reach her lips with kiss
obvious passion they're hungry to taste
the pleasure of one such as this

She leaves them shaken rattled
lives momentarily changed
there is no mistaken
she leaves them never to be the same

Queens are rare those of kind heart
helping others along the way
she plays well that part
hosting kindness helping many everyday

Chapter 9 – Reality Check

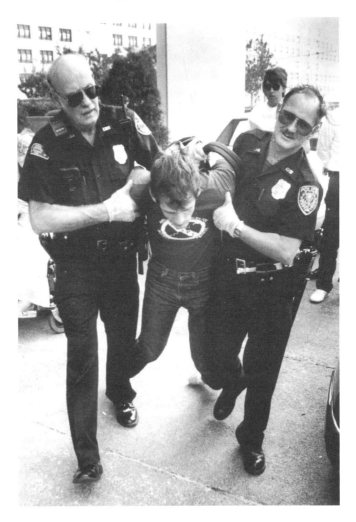

-Tom Olin

Long have you (repeatedly) experienced the death of a father... the death of a brother... the death of a sister... the death of a son... the death of a daughter... loss with regard to relatives... loss with regard to wealth... loss with regard to disease.

The tears you have shed over loss with regard to disease while transmigrating & wandering this long, long time -- crying & weeping from being joined with what is displeasing, being separated from what is pleasing -- are greater than the water in the four great oceans.

Why is that? From an in construable beginning comes transmigration. A beginning point is not evident, though beings hindered by ignorance and fettered by craving are transmigrating & wandering on. Long have you thus experienced stress, experienced pain, experienced loss, swelling the cemeteries -- enough to become disenchanted with all fabricated things, enough to become dispassionate, enough to be released."

Samyutta Nikaya XV.3
Assu Sutta

Final Incarnation

Wallowing through the uncertainty
of false righteousness
trailing fragment truth

The wind found me
dressed in awkward circumstance
moments of uncertain knowing
recognition with kindred souls

Words lead to ritual
ritual lead to remembrance
awakening I went seeking others

Reminding each other of past legend
even as we questioned our own knowing

We laugh passing time
sharing passages of favored poems
favored poets immortalized by paper

Now we come again announcing presence
with signs & wonder

Night recedes
Sunrise
on lips of morning

Mystic Fantasia

Night dark shadows narrow
contorting angles with faltering moon

Stars as elder witness
peek spectral clouds smiling in approval

I read her poems sharing insight
over spotted candlelight
words wine banter singing meaningless withdrew

She wanted so much to experience
the pledge of my prose

Glad to accommodate
the moment left us to silence
with only each other as comfort for disposition

Giving to what beckoned
I knew by her eyes that she was wanting
disposed to giving me her every secret
on sequin salver
with fingerling knot work
to highlight her jewel

Obliging I pushed her limits
exploring all angles & possibility

We converged melting into each other
intermingling auras & fate

Morning finds me with her love pressing mine
thoughts to define occasion and new poem

The Great Centering

I want them to know
wish it for them
more than anything

Not ready yet
each in own time

Long has it been
to come to this

Companion Verses

Things go unsaid
when no one cares to listen
prophets' crazy in the streets or institutions

Shut up write it down
turn back on them all
going inward

Futility ambitions
money rules world
I had to leave seek life
pervading soul to imagine

4 years I spent in Aerostar van
comforted by land
taught lesson by wind sun moon
moments alone with thought
stoned inspiration leading
parade of words

They thought me foolish
I followed curious observance
with only the remedy of words
to companion verses
ease off feeling

Born with every Sun
dying with every night
called to write
it was life for me

Thought-Filled Intending

Perceptions waver varying truth
I am in that space
where all worlds are possibility

Spirit says we must intend together harmoniously
rippling instantaneous change
allow thought to reflect higher ideals
service to one another

Bringing forth what we ourselves
magnetically project forward
Vision Thought Idea
Word Action Example
Experience Dream Reality

We are the stars of the movie
witness to every unfolding
a small miniscule tiny dirt particle part
of the greater consciousness
that birthed creation
gifting us experience
within an unbelievably vast
universe of life

Small nevertheless
our intentions are important
to balance the collective

We must perceive without judgment
see without the mind to interfere
of this great time
and the deed to be done

Reality Check

Ask yourself in this only and every moment
do I feel good right now

Is there anything
I can do differently in routine
to illicit greater pleasure
or increase happiness

What in life causes stress
and how can I transform that energy

Intent defines attraction
eliminate as much as possible
chaos hate anger pain
unless desiring such experience

Heaven is just a matter
of changing pattern
creating moment that feels good

Higher purpose will take care of higher goal
do what feels beautiful
we can allow ourselves to experience
pleasure health well being
joy happiness miracle
compassion for people
plants animals Earth and universe

My life mantra
be here now
reflecting inner witness

Sanctuary is holding life as prayer
connecting to divinity
while respecting all things as Sacred
and worthy of life

Magic surpasses the extent of reason
there is so much more to living than
culture as defined by society
science cannot explain away mystery

Analyze interaction with all energies
not just human relating
there are They that hold key
to further evolving

When the student is ready the teacher will appear

Unfolding is never guaranteed
though screenplay can channel direction

Live for purpose love
overruling other peoples expectations

Now is all that exist
become keenly aware of directing moment
responsible for the set-up
calling attraction and probability

A moment prepared in foresight
can chance an experience intended
be the creator of a movie
worthy of your life

Athens Regional Hospital
-The Great Beyond

Moments that challenge living
reclaim directive

Extreme pain presents
occasion for total clarity
where having been pushed one transcends
to something obviously further

Is it worth it to stay
endure pain to maintain connection
or would it be better for them and me
if I just let go
allow transcendence
to beyond and infinity

The only choice then
is deciding on whether to return
life experience measured

I was okay with passing
here among strangers
I felt loved

That's all people want
in final moments
to feel loved

Somebody to be present
to say goodbye world
in what would be last utterance

Near Parting

My friends family came to see me
those who couldn't called

Selective in whom I would see or talk to
even now I question
every relationship in living

I'm glad to be with my cats
last rose of summer
leaves giving up on season

I am reminded
how frail connections really are
how all things move from spring to harvest
and back again

Write like it's the last thing to ever be scribbled
last words to seduce tendency
convey feeling before
leaving for dream

We are moving into and out of duality
changing forms bodies personalities
claiming lives that sometimes make no sense

There is reason for all this cycling
greater reason than verbs allow to tell

The objective of life
Is to learn what for and why
everything then will finally make sense

Borrowed Time

Out of hospital recovered
but still something's wrong
how long until next episode

We're on borrowed time
this every moment
granted life and being
by a Creator that asks only
that we love each other
like sister brother
taking care of world
supporting every child

There are many here assisting this time
they are the miracle necessary
to set some free
allay the deepest fears of not knowing
about continuance

Assuredly I will tell you it is so
we have been since there ever was being
being is all there is ever will be
we will cross many more times in cycling

Surviving more than most can endure alone
I have shared the discourses on conscious living
exampling life as church
emphasis on holding sanctuary
in all the occasions of living
in harmony with all things
everywhere

Karma with no relating
love each other
every one around
emphasis on similarity rather than difference

Treat everyone in equal kindness
with the same regard as if
they are the last soul
you will ever see

We are guaranteed no further evolving
and there are no greater moments
than the one we occupy now

Tonight is in the Lord's hands

The Mute Genius

Quiet withdrawn the boy grunted odd sounds
in wheezing pitch
to communicate his world

It was more than his father could think to bear
or chose to see

She learned to understand him
when no one else could
deciphering lingo

She loved him decided way back
to do what she could
defiant by his side

She managed well enough alone
no one else to turn to for security
nowhere else to go
his father abandoned them both
no note he took only the money stashed
in the cupboard dish

She survived best she could
raising him on wages earned cleaning houses
him in tow

He was different early on
spent most of his life
retreating from world
to where safety protects soul

His eyes cared that nobody bothered
to contend his speech

With the IQ of a genius
it frustrated him that he couldn't move effectively
or communicate clearly

He and his mother would come to our meetings
glad others were there for them to acquaint

He's a little shy she says loosely convicted

I gave him time to ease his feeling
show him kindness without overbearing effort

Like him distant in my indifference
madly misunderstood
I promised to take him
to where the wide river falls
and the sun-drenched rainbows
are always free to see

No words need voice
sunsets humble all too same decree
free joy for taking

Net Worth

They would have you believe
that hope can no longer reach
one so fragmented in despair
dreaming to defy condition

I guess maybe that would be true
if I pitied self seriously

I just want to be able to sit without squirming
or worrying about needing to lie down

My life is just as precious
and worthy of occupation
as anybody else's no matter how important
they may think they are

I value my opportunities
things I have chance to do
with the marvel of day

I do what I feel I need
what I want
with focus attention time pursuit

I decide everyday what is relevant
for my effort and predisposition

Writing fencing reading drawing
every moment is mine
and though there are many things I cannot do
I do what I can with what I've got
and that leads me to always new possibility

Chapter 10 - The World Stands Still

- George Weld

"Human Beings and the natural world are on a collision course. Human activities inflict harsh and often irreversible damage on the environment and on critical resources. If not checked, many of our current practices put at serious risk the future that we wish for human society and the plant and animal kingdoms, and may so alter the living world that it will be unable to sustain life in the manner that we know. Fundamental changes are urgent if we are to avoid the collision our present course will bring about."

…list of crises; polluted water, oceans, soil, atmosphere, diminishing plant
and animal species and human overpopulation

"No more than one or a few decades remain before the chance to avert the threats we now confront will be lost and the prospects for humanity immeasurably diminished. We, the undersigned, senior members of the world's scientific community, hereby warn all of humanity of what lies ahead. A great change in our stewardship of the Earth and life on it is required if vast human misery is to be avoided and our global home on this planet is not to be irretrievably mutilated."

"World Scientists' Warning to Humanity"
1600 Senior Scientist from 71 countries including
over half of all the living Nobel prize winners
November 18th, 1992
The Earth Summit

4:30 a.m. 9/11/2001
- The Policeman's Wife

Early cool crisp twilight dawn
morning yet to announce arrival
new round of stars and routine

I sneak out of bed
to shower away sleep and dreams
careful to not disturb her rest
as she lies postured beneath fluttered sheets
weight of my impression upon her

4:30 a.m. and the beat calls
crime never sleeps
somewhere someone fights for life
desperate against sinister forces

Sworn to protect
I stand tall for Law & Order
awake knowing
this day could be my last

Crime will try to catch you off guard
cash in on those frail moments
where attention lags
and awareness leaves one vulnerable

She knows too and expects my arms
to cradle her form
some minutes before I leave

She wants the life of my eyes upon her
a kiss to drench our love

Duty temporarily separates our circle
I go to uphold protection and order
where I live by rules
and crime knows no limitations

I tell her I love her
it is what she wants
the words I choose to give her if all else fails

One final embrace
I step out to patrol car
& sit with thoughts of her gentle awakening
as she efforts to sleep again
restless until the comfort of my return

The World Stands Still

Cool fall day sun less brutal
sounds vary from the dark under growth
of wooded acres behind my house

Birds cicadas natural cadence
nothing takes notice
that thousands just perished in New York City

September 11th, 2001
one day before terrorists
of the 1993 world trade center bombing
were to be sentenced for first attempting
topple of the trade twins

Tatyana my overnight attendant
flips me onto my back
after a night of sleeping prone
giving butt reprieve from all day sitting

8 a.m. she leaves for school
setting me up with laptop to surf
remote for CNN and market open

Word spread online
that one of the World Trade Towers
had been hit by a commercial jetliner

I thought it a joke until
CNN showed a live shot of the second plane
gutting Tower 2 leaving both smoldering infernos
impact raining down debris
pummeling dwarf buildings cratering streets below

Like the end of the world
moment exaggerated
framed in disbelief

Flames disintegrate floors lives
in nightmare scenario
survivors crowd windows for breath
waving white flags for impossible help

People pour out in confused derision
streaming to exits
leaving friends family lovers
trapped on floors above

No where to run no escape
flame smoke heat singing lungs and body
no good conclusion could come of situation
oblivion terrorizing moments

Most had no idea
of what they were running from
or what was going on in skies above

Some leapt rather than be incinerated
by burning jet fuel
nobody could imagine such atrocity

How did this ever happen
America watched with mouths agape
tears flowing trying to compose
a shaken sense of security

II. Horizon Jewels

The twin trade towers
jewels of the New York skyline
compass for those lost in lower Manhattan
symbol of affluence and opportunity in a city
where the Statue of Liberty
stands tall to welcome immigrants
from every part of the world
are enflamed mountains of vicious red flame
and choking plumes
of thick dark black smoke

The Pentagon
center for military strategy
and intelligence gathering had also been gutted
in similar fashion
a 747 collapsing its east wall

There was news rumor that another plane
had been hi-jacked
and was heading towards another landmark in D.C.

No hope could comfort those
making last calls from that plane
passing on words of
final love and gesture

Having heard of the fate of others
passengers decided to defy the same outcome
and challenged terrorists in sinister plot
ensuring more would not die and others may live

Plane disintegrating over Pennsylvania woods
like some unwritten tragic scenario
from some Stephen King script
Tower 1 crumbled
structural steel super-heated melted
giving way to weight of higher floors

Earth-quaking implosion streaming debris
no one had a chance to run
busily assisting those
who could not get out themselves
110 stories of crushed building like dominoes
settled into three stories
of raw devastation
a 2.9 on the Richter scale

Many would be counted
among the dead today

Then just as suddenly Tower 2 crumbled
its apex falling sideways
in destructive cascade
pinnacle crushing other buildings
as it smashed earthward forced by gravity

Crushed and thrust out
as plumes of thick volcano like dust
and smoldering flame
a flutter of paper sprinkled eerily from heights
where luxury offices once stood

50,000 people were employed in those buildings
thank God & those who constructed those towers
they held for as long as they did

III. Assisting America

Volunteer citizens firefighters
police rescue workers joined
skilled and non-skilled workers
in doing what they could
to help victims and the hunt for survivors

No thought of impending danger
or concern for safety of their own
the need to help
took momentary focus away
from the smoldering inferno's
clouding sky

Some eye-witnesses said
as they were exiting floors
to run downstairs
that they saw people in wheelchairs stuck
with no way out and no one willing
to stop and assist

One lady a paraplegic
was fortunate to be carried
down 68 floors
by two men she did not even know

Once out they deposited her
at an awaiting ambulance
and went about their way
with her unsure
if they were angelic or real

One blind man was lead
by his trusty seeing eye dog
down 78 flights of stairs

Later remarking that his dog
was afraid of lightning
and other loud noises

One man knowing his best friend
since childhood
a high level quadriplegic
was too heavy
for others to care
and him to carry alone
elected to remain
until the very end
friends forever

Sunlight and CNN

For 2 weeks now I've been running
between sunlight and CNN
logging feeling
to prose for later review

Markets have declined nine percent
since trading resumed
the airline industry has lain off
20-50% of its workforce
pleading Congress for bailout

Sons daughters firefighters policeman
ambulance rescue workers
dedicated to public service
leave children behind orphaned
wives widowed husbands spouseless

Painful confusion replaces lost family members
As America honors their great contribution
understands who the heroes are
in times such as these

Our way of life has changed
never will it be the same
3000 are still missing
crushed beneath 100,000 tons
of twisted carnage remnant steel

We may never reach them all
we'll need time to come to grips
with what has occurred safety must be insured
complacent attitude forever wiped away

We will lose certain privilege
terror and propaganda
have determined we will war
freedom will insure
safety to its citizens
in the best ways that it can

Some will call for Jihad
but there is no such thing as a holy war
the two words are in contradiction

Hollywood trained our focus
on the sensational
but nobody ever expected
our national intelligence to fail

No one expected us this vulnerable

The Soft Parade Continues

13 days since the bombing of New York
and I'm still sitting
with how this tragedy
has affected and is changing my life

I've been reading literature
watching news stories media specials
and though I did not know personally
anyone that died in the tragedy

I am mourning with America
crying and weeping for people
I will never have chance to know

Time will heal wounds but never memory
tears will long be associated
to this event

We will honor the dead
assist the living bring sanity
back to their lives
in city and nation
where the Statue of Liberty
like a lighthouse holds her flaming beacon
high to horizon for all to see

We will take care of our own
always remember 9/11
a people proud recognizing peaceful diversity
honor among citizens
who respect personal freedom
rights religion individuality

America opens arms welcomingly
to all who love life
in an open-minded society
where we serve one another
for the betterment of humankind

The America I love and value
has no concern for dollars or profits
or anything other
than the well-being of its citizens

Capitalism may profess
profit at the expense of others
but the heart of America says
always be kind to others knowing
kindness one day may be needed

America is made up of
every type of person
from every nation
crossing every boundary line

Here we are more similar than different
under the American flag
we are one nation indivisible
united for the justice of all

The New America

Sure we are still in the process
of defining America today
in the midst of racial tension
disability and class difference

But 9-11 elucidated America
as all races classes' ages of people
standing or sitting in line for hours
just to donate blood
raising money for those who perished
while giving time to community and funds
aiding in the volunteer cleanup
of lower Manhattan

America is charity organizations
raising 55 million in seven days
the food service industry donating meals
and kind word to rescue workers
exhausted and hungry
devastated by what they see

Ground zero is our legacy
reminder of what the new America stands for
in the post 9-11 real world of community
and diverse integration
where we take care of one another

NFL Post 9/11

Yesterday I watched the opening ceremonies
of the first post September 11th
National Football League game
between the New York Giants
and the Kansas City Chiefs

There was a solemn feeling
that perhaps this event shouldn't go on
that the shock had not worn off enough and that
it was too soon
to celebrate moment and occasion
people were not ready
still missing those who were forcefully parted

Athletes citizens honorary fire fighters
and police rescue workers
all hailed a moment of silent prayer
to honor the heroes persons lost
to that untimely tragedy

Then we sang our national anthem
in a way I've never seen heard
or listened to before

The words will never mean
or feel the way they did then
I will never sing them
read them or be with them the same
as I did before class
during grade school ritual

Looking upon the faces
of so many proud Americans
there to celebrate
one of our nation's favorite pass times
one can see how greatly
all have been affected

Football players
honorary rescue workers
fans of all ages and races
stream tears choked up eyes wet
with pride respect for national colors
and our national song

American flags waved everywhere
jets streamed leaving trail
as people celebrated life again
honoring the dead in unity
declaring together to the world
we will go on

We will remember and we will mourn
but we will live and love
preparing our children to do the same

Al-Qaeda

A highly trained
financially backed
terror network capable
of such organized precision
must be stopped before
something worse occurs

No nation no city no people no child
will ever be safe with beings on planet
enraged enough to not have care
for themselves or anyone else

Our borders national international individual
must be managed by all people
aware of crisis situation

There is no more time for sleepwalking
the mad man challenges hero to showdown

On 9/11 there was no James Bond or Jackie Chan
to deviate criminal strategy and save the day

No nation can ever again allow jet liners
to be used as bombs by terrorists
who can successfully take over flights
with nothing more than a knife or box cutter

The need to unite and set aside difference
has been noticed
unity must spread across
boundaries and prejudice

With the success of this terror campaign
they will try further measure
to create fear in our hearts
extorting power and prejudice
sever the love which could unite our difference

In pride and wounded ego
America will retaliate
seek to honor the lives
of so many innocents lost

There will be war
God forbid weapons of mass devastation
chemical or nuclear technology
ever be used to state opinion

Or that any child should have to suffer or die
for ideas they don't understand
judgments they did not create
wars they are not responsible for

San Francisco - Dreams of Home

Near 5:30 p.m. sun drenching sky
pace of people coming and going
gathering momentum

I'm lying in the middle of the street
right outside the front entrance
of the California State Building
office of Governor Gray Davis
at the intersection of Polk and Larkin

ADAPT has surrounded
and successfully blocked off all four intersections
encompassing State Building
in protest of the rebuilding
of Laguna Honda
the nation's largest nursing home facility
housing 1200 people

Just over a month after the bombing
of the World Trade Center
by those who hate America
and its dream of freedom
I felt an awkward sense of almost guilt
for challenging the authority of our Government
in such sensitive times as these

But people are still dying
in places like Laguna Honda
gathered sardine tight
here 30 at a time in huge single room wards

Dozens will die today
Someone every 3 seconds
Existence housed in nightmare situations
deserving more than just mock freedom

Lucky to be on the outside
I feel duty to the 2.2 million people
incarcerated in nursing homes across the nation

Our Government would have us
housed in institutions
and in some States have doctors kill us
rather than fund a directive like MiCASSA
to improve the quality of life
for people elderly or with disabilities

400+ members of ADAPT chanced flying here
from all across the country to stress
how important community based services are
to our basic civil rights
and access to freedom

Laguna Honda warehouses individuals
at a cost of $330-420 dollars a day
while denying people
the one thing they truly want
choice

For what they spend
to keep people locked away
we could lavish in all sorts of luxury

II. Speaking The Unspoken

The American eagle
with wings spread on nonchalant winds
stands for freedom
the right to life liberty and pursuit of happiness

That liberty is guaranteed
by the Constitution of the United States
to all citizens without regard to race gender or age
except those born with or acquiring disability

Brooding sense of eeriness
damp low-lying clouds and light drizzle
harsh wind forcing our endurance
yesterday we in single file wrapped
around the perimeter of Laguna Honda

Like 'The Shining' this institution
had beautiful profile from the street
but could not obscure
the barred outer windows
chain linked fence blockaded by uniformed guards

Feeling of something weird going on inside
straight out of 'The World's Most Creepiest Places,'
we could not believe how many buildings
lined up row after row
behind the well-managed
manicured front lawns of main entrance

1200 people spend their every day
behind these isolation walls
looking out like ghosts haunting dream

20 minutes since the Chief of Police
warned us to move or be arrested
pressure is mounting to clear us out
so evening rush hour can resume

Hundreds of people have been looking on for hours
wondering what's up some supportive of our cause
curious on details and information
some too angry to care

Dozens of journalists scavenge stories
exclaiming to audience all we want is choice
for ourselves and those who know no freedom
having uneventful existence

As long as choice is not incorporated
into long-term care in this country
we will continue to fight gather protest
and be arrested if need be

Some here have experienced
the darkest deepest recesses of some of the shadiest
most nightmare experiences
known to American history

Tranquilizing medicine binding and shock therapy
all in the name of prescribed treatment
deemed necessary to subdue our peculiarities

They want to keep the freaks
out of mainstream
neighborhoods and schools
saving us for the circus and experimental science

III. Unlawful Assembly

Just a matter of time
before we get MiCASSA passed
and all people in nursing homes
or in danger of going
will have choice to resume community life

Hopefully soon
people with new injuries
will never have to experience the terror
of being on the verge of going into
or actually being in
a nursing home facility
without plausible alternative

Makes no sense to save us
and then warehouse us for years and years
in a place we choose not to be

We'll never disappear
Laguna Honda is proof of everything wrong
in State long-term care policy
and less than 50 miles from Berkley
home of Ed Roberts
and the first Center for Independent Living

Ed was a quadriplegic
who was denied funds because
California decided its money
would be better utilized by paraplegics
who had better opportunity of acquiring jobs
and paying taxes back to the State

Ed had to sue
just to access money set aside
for disabled students

Successful he was largely responsible
for pushing The University Of California-Berkley
into being the first
accessible American campus

Berkley also became the first city
to incorporate curb cuts on mass scale

California then became the first state to issue
a sizable grant which established
what would be
the first unofficial center
for independent living

After graduating with a PHD
Ed became head of the state department
that denied him access
to funds in the first place

Paddy wagons await our delivery
as the SFPD lifts us from the street
one by one
placing us in abandoned chairs
binding hands with plastic ties

106 of us were arrested
bodies littering the four corners surrounding
the California State Building

Picked up like discarded trash
wind strewn debris
polluting streets
we were illustrating statement
pleading for choice
voicing for millions who could not
incarcerated in institutions
across this country

We were making statement here
letting world know
this was war
and we were soldiers
expendable if need be
sacrificing self in the struggle for justice
and a victory
which would lead us
to that point
when legislation
will finally 'Free Our People'

Chapter 11 – The Bahamas Journal

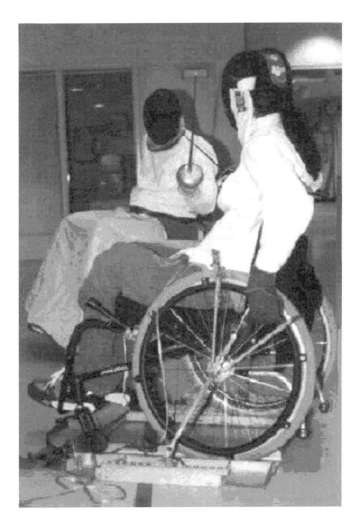

-Sandi Simpson

Now is the time of your deciding. Now is the hour of choice. You have come-as has your species-to a crossroads. You will select, in the days and weeks, months and years immediately ahead, how you want life to be on your planet-or if you want life to be on your planet at all.

This is My message to the world: You *can* create a new kind of civilization. You *can* seek a newer world. The option is yours. The moment is at hand. This is your moment of grace. Use this moment. *Seize the day*.

Begin as you awaken, by seeing yourself as Who You Really Are, by praising all that you have ever been, and all that you have become. And begin by choosing, in this moment of grace, to become more than you have ever been or ever dreamed of being; to reach beyond your own reach; to remember that nothing is beyond reach. See yourself as the light that will truly light the world. Declare yourself to be so.

Announce it to your heart, and then, *through* your heart, to everyone. Let your actions be your announcement. Fill your world with love. Know that you are the savior for whom all have waited, come to save everyone whose life you touch from any thought they may ever have that would deny the wonder of who they are, and the glory of their eternal communion with God.

–Neale Donald Walsch

Austin, Texas Summer Nationals

It's been four days of steady doing
schedule dictating that I
would spend the past three days
weaving in and out of airports
merging together a reality
that included Austin Summer Nationals
and twelve days in Freeport
with a posse of friends
more like extended family

I have progressed a great deal
dueling moments with team
highly skilled in ways of the sword

Accomplished athletes dedicated
to medals and goal
of representing country in Paralympic games

I am lucky to have access
dueling combat opportunity
with such an awesome assortment
of truly talented warriors

Nothing like sport or cause
to unify individuals
of vast background
into shared occasion

In fencing we come together
in a dialogue of swords
recognizing kindred situation
uniting us in moment

Aimless Blue Sky

Cumulus clouds wander aimless blue sky
charting direction piloting ocean blue
escorted by grand sun seated high on throne

Mango and coconut decorate native trees
easy meal for taking
hibiscus bushes vast in bloom
extend flowers everywhere
ornamenting space
in lost Eden appeal

The weather near eighty degrees year round
supports island lizards with hooked tails
darting from shade to shade
beneath the protruding undergrowth
of shabby limbed hedge

The same implications so eloquently inferred
by Bob Marley in "Crazy Bald Heads"
and "Them Belly Full But We Hungry"
applies to the Bahamas as well

Selective slavery still exists on mass scale
catering to influx of vacationing tourists
furthering reach of colonial conquest

The World Trade Organization
established a Global 'free'-market system
which offers money to those
willing to rape Earth of commodity

It's all just a ploy to support
corporate monologue
protection of territory and interests

Money rules intention idol God
people will turn on
friends family loved ones
just to climb the 'well to do' ladder

Souls sold reaching top
hungry to acquire new items
'necessary' for living
people have all but forgotten life
before modern convenience

The sun rises in slow presentation
clouds push wave and wind
quietly nature redeems abandoned buildings
reclaiming glory in erosive harmony

Everything given so freely
always is
delivered into her grasp again

Paradise Isle

The islands have always eluded me
Ocean mother ancient emerald friend
aquatic gardens a womb of leisure

Paradise coves lined in drift sands
surround island morsel
depths hide untold myths
the rise and fall of civilizations peoples
history billions of legends long

Atlantis is rumored
between Bimini and Cuba
a lingering vortex
vestige of failed merkaba
13,000 years ago in resulting destruction

The crush blue covers
monumental temples
and an unrequited story
of illusive past

Waves sparkle diamond crest
jeweled moon as consort
reflects sun
ancient witness to a history of deluge
and polarity reversal

Remnants of immortality
we are particles of a forgotten past
souls condensed falling freeform
like raindrops attesting life's duality

In lesson with others seeking reprieve
descending mountains chasing rivers
crashing dam for release

We are eager to do
what natural mystic intends

They can't keep us caged any longer
rainbows mark our fall
auroras crawl sky
a hint to others
never forget it was all fated
the story of our coming
signs of quickening
drops leading to paradise ocean
sooner or later

Glitter Stars Casting Night

Glitter stars height of night
I write because it feels right
you're nowhere to be seen

Words fill feeling with meaning
memories appealing
drift and abound

I failed you the love we'd found
lost in the crowd
of you approaching near

From nowhere
your visage appeared and I gasp
smiling with ghost laugh
as I'd engage you in conversation
declarations of how you made me reel
feel both shy and alive

Lips given to teasing one another
lovers we needed no other
to grace each flutter of provision

A decision I always knew
look forward to
and was sure to let you know
maybe a little too much so

It was hard to let you go
needing a kiss before you went away
then driving myself crazy for days
trying to keep all this love in

Like sin when you must confess
or butterflies before a test
you made me high
touching me so deeply
I didn't know why
it was sort of creepy
how affected I was
by your presence in my life

And even though I wanted
to make you my wife
it was either lose myself and stay
or elect to walk away

And I did though
I could never deny
your soft reply or words you'd say
feel of soft sky when we play
gentle love made our way
and the eventual fall
to Earth again

Chosen Hero Role

Those who have carried vision
from untold worlds
through stranger space than words
can allow to tell

Call for healing
filling moment with meaning
sending vibration to trigger
change for self and globe

There are many now
who understand things once unspeakable
able to anchor in new direction
while giving reflection
to the renewed interest
in higher aspects of consciousness

We are close new sign enters our spheres
final 9 years of Mayan Codex
Aquarius and beginning of next
25,870 year cycle

Our grand sun triggered a brilliant firestorm
auroras haunt skies in warm visceral hue
faster vibrations influx new gifts
for those who are able to handle
an intensely transmutable experience

Some things are not yet meant to be shared
even willingness does not denote
one ready to comprehend meaning
leading it to this

Many are plunging into awaiting abyss
honoring obligation to chosen hero role
claiming themselves as living legend
that will someday be lost mythology

Forever will we play dancing through eternity
with friends & fortune
teaching each other one another
about what's to come
but more importantly what is

I am rambling making sense to me
are you lost in my words-
Do you not see
the sparkle of realization
memory too that indwells
the far corridors
of your own souls knowing

Think me crazy but these words
are for those them that know
who feel beyond doubt of what I speak

Come with me
I will light our attachment to each other
measure our similarities
rather than focus on difference

Truth imbues soul
knowing is always available
unnecessary to hermit
ice topped snow capped mountains
meditate frigid waterfalls in searching Nirvana

Lightning That Thunders Storm

I am that lightning that thunders storm
I am Omega before Alpha born
I am the serpent swallowing tail
I am promise prophesizing no fail

I am the trees birds and breeze
I am the weather that does what it please
I am the night that comforts day
I am dreams inviting souls to play

I am the mystery holding all at once
I am calendar with thirteen moon months
I am the fairy that beckons your call
I am the spark that ties you to all

I am the orbits guiding ellipse
I am the moon/sun in perfect eclipse
I am the mirror reflecting guise
I am the spark seen in smiling eyes

I am the comet wandering wide space
I am the challenge testing our race
I am the shadow that follows our sun
I am the duality that says we are all one

I am is was will ever be
I am then now all eternity
I am you and you are me
Together we make up the greatest mystery

Clouds Obscuring Sun

You never know people
until you spend
extended durations of time
being witness
to their routine quirks and behaviors

People can rally up a game face
to play certain role
but eventually
masks come down
and what was covered
with ornamentation
is no longer veiled by disguise

What is revealed is sometimes
only lies
clouds obscuring sun

I Have Come In Defense Of My Mother

I have come in defense of my mother
to honor the life she has given me
Where are my other brothers
to aid in protecting thee?

She bleeds freely wounded by hate
where are they she has loved?
Where are those who can appreciate
for them all that she has done?

I can't watch her cry
and not be affected by her pain
I must take stand by her side
for I she'd do the same

I have come in defense of my mother
I can't let you pollute her sacred ground
Lo, when I heard it was you my brother
I thought them joking around

The Days Between

The sun will disappear in 30
night acquaint encroaching skies

I came to this place to honor
chill moments with her
somewhere out there also stargazing
her own memories of our parting

I see her coming even now
riding moonbeams in hippy grace

Somewhere she watches evening for inspiration
seeing me in crystal ball
forging words on her behalf

Before incarnating we promised
at all costs to find each other
fate we said would guide
our parting heaven's throne

Holding onto memories as conscious faded
birth strange armor of soul
callous veil of forgetting

For 30 years I wandered
a gypsy scribe
loose upon garden paradise
shaking off the spell of new cycle

Entrenched in confused scenario Babylon tyranny
doctrine of law regulated
by souls more lost than me

It was 10 years ago
I woke to full remembrance
seeking her ever since

Long have I carried
the secret of ancient metaphor
longing for the leisure
of her gentle spaces

I am watching even now
unfolding paths waiting
the reward of her eyes

Completion for no other but me
it has been what seems lifetimes
since I've tasted her in form
soul-mate the link
to accomplish me further
than the lone seeker is allowed to go alone

I see her parting trail
lighting incense in her prayerful way
new cycle beginning
moments ripe for her return

Soon all things revealed to knowing
she will remember too in time
if not already

Greater destiny mixing lives
and the design of fortune
another sunset claimed by distant trees
tear sheathed in longing

Somewhere she sings
songs to empty ghosts
summer clouds cradle
her chalice form

I wait out the storm
and miss her
like breathe the dying man
offering empty words
to sway of ocean horizon
hungry for her return

Rhyme Flow

I know why I never write in rhyme anymore
takes too much time thought to define
meaning of each precarious line
when each word is wine door for poetry

Rhyme seems a tedious sort of chore
trying to set up specific ending
give significance to words depending
on what sound image they convey
limited to how they play out on page
slave to certain word dependence
adjective adverb verb plotted in precise space
of sentence

Sometimes too much thought
hinders channeling message
being vessel for flowing story
each word carries glory or worry
depending on plea
each a seed to flower unfolding need
shower those who read
heeding in deliberate chase
like all or one holding everything
in single syllabic embrace

A holographic universe
everything found in content of every atom
every thought one can fathom
found in each piece of the whole
that's how I write now
with wow in every word

If I do rhyme its part of flow
but don't expect
that's how it will go
suppose I die
as I write a line of a song
or my reader dies as their reading along

Would I invest all interest in only
the ending word of poem
or in every flow of its going

No one knows when end will come
and besides it is not about the sum
but the math along the way
promised no further days
I play each as it comes

Wherever I May Roam

Wherever I go
I'm fully aware of being there
even when I don't go anywhere
at all

Home is where conscious is
where life always gives you
all you could want
or thought you'd need

Like wisdom in words you read
inspiring feeling and good deed
service to humankind
blessing to those in mind

I find no matter where one insists to go
conscious knows
nothing exists but here

No there being in future or past
to anchor in moment
evading center
mentor of personal laws
seeking effect before cause
when in truth there is only
the pause breathing in between

Acquainting New Story

I missed you though you'd never know
I had to kiss you then let you go
hoping someday you'd return again

More than just a friend
able to mend acquainting new stories
of ventures apart space to fury mark new start

Don't forget I loved you and still do
it was not your fault we grew through
different fates at different rates
making mistakes that settled
our relationship in doom

Maybe we met too soon
I was growing too fast and you
you needed time to grasp
what in end would be
remedy to free the best of one another

Always feel free to call
I wish nothing but the best for you
it's all I ever meant to do I guess
though sometimes I failed honoring self instead
I was blessed to have led life to this
you were a gift of destiny

Before I go might I have one more kiss
as I leave on my way
love you hope to see you again someday
until then it was good to know you

For Minna

I see her coming conjuring comfort
answering riddles
of a thousand just like me

She was not in seek of this
none of us were
content in owning all pleasure
every leisure ours for attempting

It doesn't matter how it happened
what fates lead course
it changes nothing
of dependence on wheeled chariot

What matters is that she's here
available to console her children
and those who soothe her own tears

Struggling initially
who doesn't plunging depths
cast on hell's gates forced to fight off demons
or be dragged inside

Busy living again doing the work
that is her sacred dream
finding meaning in the simple
others can't know for her
enlightening purpose on this plain

Shepherd's peer support director
diving oracle shedding light for others
seeking enchanted company

I watch her unveil secrets
bearing personal mythology
lesson to others
in need of her song

Beacon for others peering through dim
in need of honing light
to impose direction

She is the north star
guiding others' progress
harbor from which navigation is possible
Polaris declaring
this way leads home

One day I will see her again
in some never-ending lifetime
as yet unmentioned
where we are not needed for this change
where we can just be witness
to all grandeur consciousness composes

It is written in the heavens
encrypted in starshine
gods and goddesses know story
prophecies explain tale
of them that were sent
to experience different
shedding all karma
to know grace worthy of surrender

The Bloodline Restored

I know it couldn't have been
easy for you trying to
define yourself growing up
through broken homes
and fathers who could never
claim you as their own

Thank you Justin
for embracing uncertainty
without question of where
have I been all your life

I could never justify that answer
I could never even try

You coming back into my life
is and has been
the greatest event of my years

I will honor you first
in all the things that I do
trying always to take care
of your wants and needs
in regard to my own

You already are so much more
of a man than I ever was

I hope to live up
to the standard you have set
hoping only to mirror
the lesson you present me

Young master of so much already
proficient with pen skateboard wakeboard
keyboard bass and guitar

Those around you
will look to you to lead

Guide them well
as I support you
in the things
that make you
a great blessing to world

Know that everything I do
the sum of all I am and will be
is for you son without question

New Year Confidant

She came to me in dream
I saw her the next day
Not letting opportunity slide
I went to her to say
hey I don't know you
but saw you in a dream
thinking this a pick-up line
she didn't say a thing

Detecting some scene
of her own lingering dream
she said I can't place exact space
but I remember your face as well
I can't yet tell but know of what you mean

I said I've seen your face before as well
I don't remember exactly how
memories may yet tell
the deja-vu of this moment now

I said I can't recall the details of that dream
or what exactly they mean
but feel the same thing
and I didn't want to seem sly
but only try to abide
whatever connection may remain

She said it's hard to explain
it's such a weird thing
but I am glad we had a chance to meet
chance to greet this strange space
able to taste whatever may yet grace outcome

After talking awhile
she gave me her number
and I went along my way
we promised to meet
share dinner later in the day

I was excited to explore
whatever fate may hold for us in store
recognition dawns the eye
no coincidental meeting
moments though fleeting
are like that in mystery
never know just go and see
feel things out as one goes along
find a niche in which one belongs
sharing whatever may come
of this lesson in duality

And So It Is

We have no idea where future leads
or what present awaits our flaccid embrace
we only have choice to make decision
move on regardless of odds
or death awaiting admission to just succumb
there will be them later counting on us
to make it to achieve survival now

There will be they
who need our experience of evolution
who will later lean on our will to survive
and push themselves onward facing that day
when they too conquer experience
that will enable someone else to help themselves

There are grandparents parents siblings children
dependent on our decisions
in these fragile times before us now
what role we choose to assume
will decide the future glories
of nations civilizations cultures generations
that will one day seek
to achieve what seems to us now miracle outcome

Neither deny self the full capacity
of the experience before you
but recognize that saving yourself
in these crucial moments gives others chance
to save what may be the something or someone
who will one day save another's world or universe
as it is when the butterfly flutters waves resonate
echoing through dimensions rippling great change

We are seeds planted planting our own
for what will be garden someday
our children's children
will finish wherever we may fall short
accomplish where we may fail
press on where we have retreated

We are each the story
which one day becomes legend
each the hero accomplishing miracle feat
in each of our genes the prophet parables mystery
fantasy becomes real uncertainties become known
and the known becomes the stuff of mythology

We are born into exact circumstance
necessary for evolving soul
for this lifetime will make or break
who we have chance to become
no coincidences no perchance happenings
everything is exactly as it was supposed to be
or it would not

The only thing we can control
the only thing we can direct
is individual free will and how to use it
those lucky enough to have sober understanding
of how awesome and beautifully miracle
each moment of life is
are the saviors heroes oracles
gods goddesses remembered
for not what they said but how they were
everyone else will be just a word on the page
of the great story that is life
and so it begins…

The Rising Possibility Of A Forever Moment

Excitement ensues dimming lights
New Year's Eve could be no better
than at concert with Tanja Avery and thousands
collectively intending peace and good time

As the filtering flow of people
seeking assigned seat came to halt
I took notice of her
a dreamy sort of sultry hip chick
directly in front of me one row down
and choice benediction for espying eye

Eased in with acoustic mix
Widespread set it off right
exuding sweet discourse
to enchant night in pleasing melody

The end of 2003 everyone fully hyped
the fury of dance articulated appreciation
as every anthem was hailed in shouts of merriment

Fans befriending others around
share more than just meaningful conversation
with those acquainting story

I watched her spin writhe and turn
owning space ruling movement
hips a squall of beat
feet a clamor of rhythm
in intoxicating display

Night prevailing occasion found our stares
drifting stares at each other
prolonged glance courted invitation
interest met and all else faded

Spellbound feeling grip
she came to me floating steps in temple rise
settling to occupy space by my side
presence like sunrise on a beach
of warm comfort
sky in shock color lending spectacle
awesome to witness

Daring to convey attraction
we spoke in gentle slang engaging review
attempting to solve riddle persuading curiosity

I will never forget the feel of her check
skin brushing mine as we exchange dialogue
lending ear to pass sentiment
above the stirring echoes
of crowd resolute in having good time

Pressing night passing word
her hair glistening damp from celebration
glimpsed my shoulders
as she lean in to whisper reply
bartering questions confirming appeal

Several times our lips nearly brushed
as we offered words to display
detail of life and going

There was reason for she and I to meet
this realized as Encore spun into 'Vacation'
'I didn't see you were right next to me
but I'm so glad you could make it
with you by my side I might get back alive
from my next Vacation'

Our lips pressed in gentle kiss
eyes locked staring lengths at each other
lost in her ocean blue
I embraced the mood of this moment
and our coming together

No goodbye to story
morning dawned with visions
of her gypsy eloquence
still fresh in mind
trying not to wake
and lose her in parting

I smiled warm inside
touched by
the rising possibility of a forever moment

Babylon and Beyond

Leave the rotten towns of your father,
the poisoned wells of blood stained streets,
enter now the sweet forest
- Jim Morrison

Yashuah disappeared for 20 years
before reemerging to contemporary eye
rumors say he went East
lulled by merchant talk
& myth of God sized temples

I left too straddling contemptuous winds
chasing elusive sun to ocean horizon
where it would leave me defeated
with only Venus night
as comfort to assess my disposition

We must all leave
at least once to understand condition
there are whole towns in the West
full of those that have escaped

Paid to surf skyscraper mountains
from Sunrise to Sunset everyday
in a place where Internationals vacation

Public opinion thinks enlightenment
contained in books
law communally
backed by certifiable teachers

The Native Americans
went to the desert vast in religion
humbled for communion
seeking vision unique to circumstance

The grand palace didn't understand
laughed at young Buddha
when he renounced his crown
dropping imperial arrangement
turning back on myriad
friendly lovers of royalty

Seeking answer he offered crown jewels
radiant in cascading glow
to beggars fallen to destitution
and exclaimed to world
"Take all that I have which conspires mind
when nothing remains for fingers to snatch
there you will find me dressed in nakedness
seeking that which physical cannot offer"

Parting Word

-Tom Olin

I decided to add this addition to the book to capture where we are this moment in disability history. I wrote the following 2 articles for the September and November 2003 issues of Disabled Dealer Magazine, covering two of the most important issues affecting people with disabilities living in America now, community based services and physician assisted suicide.

One promises to uphold our right to healthy, empowered, inclusive lives in a culture which honors differences in ways of being. The other challenges our right to life of some, based on economics and others opinion of whether we as people with disabilities deserve the right to live or not.

ADAPT is in the forefront of the community based services issue as well as many other issues while NOT DEAD YET is leading the drive to ensure our entitlement to our own lives. ADAPT is close to getting MiCASSA passed into law with the backing of the Supreme Courts' Olmstead vs. LC/EW case, upholding Title II of the American's with Disabilities Act, concerning our right to lives in community in the 'most integrated setting.'

With the ongoing Terri Schiavo case, battle lines have been drawn for NOT DEAD YET and the right to deny lifers. It has taken the work of hundreds of advocates across the country working daily to push for change in current legislation and now we are so very close to decisions which will dawn a beautiful new chapter of history.

MiCASSA March/Rally

-Tom Olin

ADAPT is celebrating the 20th anniversary of its first action by marching 144 miles from the Liberty Bell in Philadelphia, Pennsylvania to Capitol Hill in Washington, D.C. The march is in honor of people everywhere in this Nation who wish, need, want alternatives to the current long term care bias favoring nursing homes and institutions.

Dubbed the Free Our People March and Rally of 2003, this event promises to be one of the most significant examples of self-determination by any oppressed group in the history of the Americas. People will literally be sacrificing themselves, body and health to show to the world that we are serious about the cause of freedom. 120 people, many using wheelchairs and other mobility aids, from many states across the U.S. will begin the march in Philadelphia, to be additionally joined by 80 others in Baltimore, to cover the last half of the march to Washington, D.C.; which will then culminate in a planned 20,000 people gathering at Capitol Hill to demand the passage of MiCASSA (S. 971 and H.R. 2032).

Why is it important that we support ADAPT and the Freedom March/Rally for MiCASSA? One very simple and important reason is that ADAPT is fighting for the quality of everyone's life in America. With the recent cuts happening in the Medicaid budgets of every state, long term care programs that are alternatives to nursing homes will be the first to be slashed as expendable services.

With the bias in our nation towards institutions, programs such as the Independent Care Waiver or the Community Care Services Program are coined "optional" programs and not necessary for the Medicaid program to survive as a 'whole.' Nursing homes and institutional care, however, are slated 'necessary' and therefore 'mandatory' to Medicaid expenditures. What this means is that nursing homes are guaranteed that money will be there for their services, whereas alternatives to institutionalization may or may not find states budgeting money for their needs. It does not matter that the national average has 85% of long term care Medicaid dollars going to nursing homes and institutions.

What is happening now in states is that legislatures are trying to save money by slashing funds from the 15% budgeted for alternatives to institutions. These programs allow the aging and disability communities to live life involved in the culture, with ability to make self-actualized choices dictating things like - What time do I want to get up today? What do I want to eat today? Do I want to go anywhere today? Do I want friends over today? Do I want to take a bath today? What will I do today? Do I want to work on a project today or just rest and chill? Do I want to read or hang out with friends today? Simple things like this are what's important in creating quality of life for people that would not otherwise have it should they be in an institutional setting where 2 people are responsible for taking care of the wishes and needs of 20 to 30 people.

There is no possible way that 2 people can cater to even 5 to 10 people's wants and needs without someone being neglected. Nursing homes routinely tell their employees to take on the task of trying to comfort 15 to 30 people. Employees automatically know they cannot in any way accomplish such task and the real question for them is not whether they can do it or not, but who can they push off enough to get what they can do accomplished. What that means for patients is that often basic needs will be ignored to the point that many will not get to bathe in any way, decide what time they want to get up or even whether they get up. Life outside of the nursing home is almost non-existent unless there is a rare community outing.

With the Independent Care Waiver or Community Care Services people are encouraged to make and take upon themselves all of the decisions which truly make life worthy of living. We as the recipients of these services are just people who have aged or acquired disability in such a way that we need the services of others to maintain lifestyle. This does not make us criminals and we should not be treated as such. Services that empower our independence should not be viewed as 'optional' by our government when services that lock us up in often nightmarish circumstance are viewed as 'mandatory', but they are. Budget cuts threaten alternatives to institutionalization when in my mind 85% of the long term care budget should go to waiver and community care programs that should be 'mandatory' and institutions should get only 15% and be seen as 'optional'.

We the people are the only buffer between the decisions and legislations that continue to keep things the way they are with most of the long term care budget going to institutional supports which rob people of identity and dignity. If you think this doesn't affect you because you are not in need of either community or institutional supports now, I guarantee if you live long enough that you will be someday. Why not help us to vote to make things right now, so that should you or family members ever need such support, that the network will be in place to serve you or them in a way that insures health and quality of life.

That is the reason why ADAPT is holding this March/Rally; to ensure quality of life for every American citizen regardless of race, gender, religion, etc. ADAPT is trying to help everyone and we need your aid, to aid America. Please register to vote, if you have not and seek a relationship with your political representatives. Know what they are doing and assure that they know what you want them to do for you. If we all become aware of what's going on in Washington D.C. and our state capitols, they will not be able to perpetuate cycles which hold us as victim. We can then in turn, come together in number to guarantee that the elected officials know that we know what they are up to, and that if they do not represent us and our wishes, that they absolutely will be without a job. That is the only way we can affect change in this country, insuring that what is passed as law, qualifies as the will of the people, in service of the common good.

As we come to the end of the millennium, we are at a crossroads that forces us to choose between two mutually exclusive value systems. Will we remain on the trail that leads ultimately to the full realization of the equality-of-human-life ethic and with it, the tremendous potential for the creation of a true community, or do we take a hard turn down the slippery slope toward a coarsening of our views of the afflicted, the dying, the chronically ill, the disabled, and those in pain or depression to the point where we feel they have a duty to die and get out of the way?

To put it more bluntly; Will we choose the road of inclusion and caregiving for all, including the weakest and most vulnerable among us, or that of exclusion and ever-expanding killing opportunities? More simply yet: Will we choose to love each other or abandon each other? The bottom line: Will we keep or lose our empathy? The two paths that lie before us, the death culture or the struggle toward a truly caring community, lead to dramatically different futures. The choice is ours. So will be the society we create.

Wesley J. Smith

Terri Schiavo Survives Nightmare

-Tom Olin

Behind closed doors in hospitals, hospices and nursing homes, conscious people with disabilities, old and young, are being deprived of food and water, in the absence of a living will or other clear and convincing evidence that they would choose this for themselves. This is being done based on physicians' predictions and judgments about present and future quality of life, predictions and judgments that numerous research studies prove are scientifically unreliable, negative and inconsistent with the views of people with disabilities ourselves. Disabled people know that we can't count on the courts to protect us against a doctor or family member who feels that we would be better off dead or they would be better off without us.

The Schiavo case should be seen as a wake up call for all of us. This case is about officially and permanently dismantling the constitutional rights of people who have guardians and giving carte blanche to guardians to starve and dehydrate people who are seen as not worth the effort or expense. Disability rights groups are coming forward to argue that it's time to reestablish constitutional protections against a health care system that's been putting profits before people for far too long. We deserve an honest public debate before we grant the health care system a virtually unfettered right to kill.

-Diane Coleman

Terri Schiavo Survives Nightmare

There has always been one group of people with power to control outcomes for another; treating them depending on how they viewed them. Those who have authority to make decisions, impose rules laws regulations, but do not always take into consideration what is necessarily good for those for whom decisions are made. On Aug. 22, 2003 a seven-member Florida Supreme Court unanimously refused to review Terri Schindler Schiavo's case and sent it back to probate court. Judge George Greer scheduled a hearing for Sept. 11 to set date for removal of her feeding tube.

On February 25, 1990 Terri, age 26, suffered massive brain damage when she collapsed at her home under unexplained circumstances. She suffered cardiac arrest and slipped into a coma. When she came out two months later, she was severely brain damaged and unable to walk, talk, or eat. This has lead to a decade long battle between Michael Schiavo, her husband and legal guardian, and her parents, the Schindlers. On Sept. 2, 2003, U.S. District Judge Richard A. Lazzara, in Tampa scheduled an emergency session when Michael Schiavo ordered his wife Terri removed from a hospital where she was being treated for a severe infection to a hospice before she had been stabilized of her condition. Two weeks prior Terri was taken to the same hospital because she was coughing up blood and appeared to have aspiration pneumonia. She was returned to the hospice less than a week later, again before she had fully recovered.

Florida Governor Jeb Bush intervened on her behalf because he was "disturbed" by rumors of Michael Schiavo's actions related to Terri's current care. He wrote a letter to Judge Greer requesting a delay in removal of Terri's feeding tube until certain issues were investigated. He specifically cited Michael's request to disallow treatment. Bush urged Greer to ensure that "no act of omission or commission be allowed to adversely affect Mrs. Schiavo's health before the September 11th hearing you have set. No one involved should be permitted to circumvent due process or the court's authority in order to achieve personal objectives in this case."

Michael Schiavo, her husband, in a 1992 malpractice trial was awarded by jury $1.3 million dollars. Of that money, Michael received $300,000, lawyers' fees paid, and about $750,000 put in trust to pay for Terri's rehabilitation. Because Terri's insurance had run out, the need to restart therapy was used by Michael to persuade jury into settlement. However, once the money was in the bank, Michael deprived Terri of any kind of rehabilitation and even placed a "do not resuscitate" order on her chart. He denied her antibodies several times when she had life threatening infection and even barred Monsignor Thaddeus Malanowski, Terri's Catholic priest from seeing her and performing Sacraments.

Michael claims that Terri would not have wanted to live this way and is determined to have her feeding tube removed. He hired right to die lawyers to aid him in persuading the court systems that removing

Terri's feeding tube and allowing her to starve and dehydrate for 10-14 days until she dies, is the best thing for her. He insists that he loves her anytime anyone from media, TV, radio, or newspaper calls for an interview, and yet never voluntarily mentions that he lives with his new fiancé and has 2 children by her, or that they have been together for 8 years. Neither does he mention that only about $50,000 of the $1.3 million dollars won in Terri's malpractice suit, has been used on Terri's behalf in the five years following the jury verdict. Since 1998, Michael Schiavo has expended $650,000 not for therapy, but primarily for lawyers in his efforts to see Terri killed.

Over a dozen prominent doctors and therapists have stated that with therapy she could be rehabilitated, against three doctors who maintain she essentially is comatose and will never recover. This case challenges the right to life and quality care of every person born into and alive now in America. Should someone deem you unworthy of life, the consequences can be a horrific. Even now in hospitals across the nation, parents are told that babies born with deformation, mental or physical disabilities are not worthy of life and that their only hope would be to live all their days in nursing homes or mental institutions. They then get parents to consent to removing babies from life support systems that allow children to die from dehydration or starvation. Babies are literally allowed to cry, whine, and beg for nourishment that they are denied because our society does not value children or people with disabilities.

Terri's parents the Schindlers have been battling their son-in-law over the care and custody of their daughter. They want Terri's guardianship transferred to them so that they can look after her well being and provide for her the measures that would assure her further joy and happiness in life. Michael Schiavo refuses to grant them guardianship because he is intent on seeing her executed. The question remains- Why is it so important for him to have Terri die? Is it the money he stands to gain from her death or it something more?

Could it be that he is responsible for her current condition and does not want her to be rehabbed to the point that she could speak or communicate in some other way that perhaps he tried to harm her and is in truth responsible for her current condition? Why, won't he allow Terri speech or cognitive therapy, or just go on with his life and his new family?

He has time and time again refused anyone to assist Terri in anything that might better her prolonged outlook on life. Why not just allow her parents, who love her dearly, to take over her care. It seems to me if he loved her so that he would allow her parents and others to try and do all they could for her. Why then would he fight so hard to be allowed to subject her to death by starvation and dehydration unless he has something to hide, and Terri's death means secret kept. We may never know but surely something is amiss.

On Oct. 15, Judge George Greer, a federal circuit appeals court judge sided with Michael Schiavo and allowed her feeding tube to be removed and the countdown to Terri's horrible bout begin. Had it not been for disability and right to life advocates across the country imploring the media blitz that brought national attention to her plight, Terri might not have survived the ordeal that disconnected her from life supports for 6 very cruel days. It could have been her execution by a justice system that is supposed to protect and uphold the rights of citizens subject to its laws. This judicial system would have failed her in an atrocious manner had we not bombarded the Florida legislature and Governor Jeb Bush with phone calls and email requests to stop this horrible deed set to take place. Terri had done nothing to deserve such cruel and unusual punishment and we could not just stand by and let it happen.

It was Oct. 20, 2003, time was of necessity, conditions extremely urgent that an emergency session of Florida legislatures met, proposing "Terri's Law." At 10:10 p.m. the House passed the bill. 3:30 p.m. Oct. 21, the Senate passed the bill with revisions. 4 p.m. the House gave final approval and at 4:30 p.m. Governor Bush signs the bill into law. In less than 24 hours, "Terri's Law," gave the Governor authority to place a moratorium on the dehydration deaths of certain cognitively disabled patients, including Terri. And finally, at 9:15 p.m, Terri was given fluids and resumed eventual feeding.

She nearly died, forced to endure nightmare experience, while family and advocates looked on hoping that some miracle would come into play and save her innocent life. Her father and mother were forced to witness the gravity of it all and could not believe their daughter was having her life extinguished by law and court opinion. I have watched over time, written articles, commentary to news publications, legislatures, and television shows about Terri's right to quality in life, so when word was first sent of Judge Greer's decision to allow her death I was initially shocked and then later appalled. I could not believe that Judges in our State and Federal judiciary systems, held such views as to disregard people with disabilities any kind of worth or belief that we would want to live in condition different than the assumptions of 'normality.'

In our history, people with disabilities have been denied every kind of right, life, liberty, and happiness one can imagine. Our government and culture has overlooked our most basic right to quality in life, access to community, jobs, public transportation, housing, entertainment, education, as well as the most basic accommodation to such as bathrooms or entrance into homes, businesses while at the same time sending us to institutions and facilities that under-mind our basic integrity, freedom, choice, will. They have placed us at the mercy of experimental science and medicine that would legally inflict brutish treatments such isolation, binding, electric shock, and drug therapy just to subdue our peculiarities.

And now there is growing sentiment to allow physician assisted suicide in instances of want or necessity as decided by guardians, family, doctor, or circumstance. Isn't the Hippocratic oath about saving lives. I think more what needs to be considered is why people would want to kill themselves or why circumstances would lead some to want or wish for suicidal measure. I feel what would be seen is that people do not want to live lives involved with high degrees of pain, loneliness, or in settings where they are allowed no control of decisions which affect them, or in places that do not care for them in a healthy, quality of life promoting way.

As it stands now Michael Schiavo is appealing the right of the Governor to step in and prevent Terri's death by starvation, dehydration. However, the Federal court has granted petition to hear motion to remove Michael Schiavo from guardianship citing abuse, neglect, and adultery. Circuit Judge George Greer, who has primarily handled this 10-year court battle between Michael Schiavo and the Schindlers; has consistently ruled in favor of Michael Schiavo, but recently denied request by Schiavo's attorney to dismiss the motion. The case is still not over with deliberation going back and forth. Everyone please include Terri and the Schindlers in your prayers and may justice do the right thing.

Acknowledgements

Always first praise to the Creator, Creation, Great Spirit within and all around, for every breath, blessed moment of life, everything that is was will ever be. Honor to Earth, Sun, Moon, Keepers of the Book of Life, Dream Teachers, Ancestor Spirits, Ascended Masters. No amount of word could ever grant praise enough for the pleasures of conscious knowing. Grateful I am to have opportunity to do part in the great change that is before us now. Long has it taken to get here.

To all of my relations, elders everywhere responsible for the bloodlines of all peoples. Special honor to my Grandmothers and Grandfathers, Cristina and Pete Garcia, Kim Lyang J. and Shin Gi When, who together passed on the seed birthing our generations, had it not been for their love siring bloodlines and raising children, we would not, could not in turn raise our own.

Special honor to my Mother and Father, Manuel Pedro and Myong Hwa Garcia, no better parents could I have chosen for guidance in this realm, so much love I have for you for always loving me unconditionally, and accepting me for who I am, and have willed to be. Thank you both for exemplifying to me what great parents are and for always doing what you could in proving you love me so. It has been beautiful sharing this life with you in the evolution of a parent child.

Love and respect to my surrounding family for every extended courtesy, for always supporting my endeavors, Patrick and Nam Sun (Jodi) Gannon, Samantha and Vernon Kiernan, Elva and Leroy Gonzalez, Lucy and Manny Sanchez, Billy and Norma Jane Garcia, Jimmy and Chris Garcia, Delores Garcia; cousins Patrick and Leah Gannon, Annette Rodriguez, Ray Garcia, Renee Garcia, Julie Fields, Donna Zackery, Tina Patrick, Peggy Garrison, Roberta Smith, Billy and Lori Garcia, Natasha Marquez and extended family in New Mexico, Korea, and elsewhere.

Special praise to my son Justin James Garcia and mother Stacy Yates, for their beautiful incorporation into my world and the wonderful lesson, joy they bring to my life. No better fate could have been bestowed my way. Justin, thanks son for meeting me in the middle, and being so willing to endeavor new relating. You are my greatest joy. Stacy, I can't say enough to you kind sister, for bearing my seed, being there through thick and thin, and being so overly cool about always granting me new chance. I am thrilled that we have new opportunity to unfold the next chapter of our story together as one large extended family.

To Ray Yates, I can't ever thank you enough for encouraging Justin and Stacy in their pursuit to re-establish ties with me, when others only sought to hinder our circle. You are a huge part of why all is harmonious now. I am indebted to you more than I can ever hope to repay. If you ever need of me for anything, just ask and I'll do my very best to help.

To Bert and Cynthia Taylor, Charles, Sherri and Terri, for accepting me without reservation or question, and always receiving me without condition. Thanks for caring for Justin all these years with the kindness that makes us family.

For the many people who have worked for me in and out of the cycle of years, all of you are so very important to me, you will never know how much I love you and appreciate your service, the best of friends, without you I could not have even delivered this now in your honor- Nakisa Glenn, Brenda Crayton, Angel Deason, Kerrie Trammel, Pam Walls, Amanda Ellsworth, Tracy Stricklan, Heather Hays, Tanja Link, Tatyana Kalininchencko, Reannon Wright, Summer Young, Britney Buck, Tiffany Hyland, Sarah Gromel, Nora Fitzpatrick, Bethany Walsch Smith, Katherin Shore, Priscilla Bugari, Taylor Canterbury and Adrienne Cooke.

To old and new friends who have stuck by my side through-out my unfolding, I owe you more than I will ever be able to lay claim, bless you for truly exampling relationship- Pat and Kim Murphy, Avery Cotton, Jeff Jones, Chris McMurray, Jacquelyn Howard, Bill Fleming, Brett and Valerie Vallaincourt, Carrie Butts, Anne Dee Ackerman, Tyrone Johnson, Wesley Pope, Bart Floyd, Basil and Tami Youman, Andreena Patton, Jennifer Melton, Angel and Kevan Knowles, Trena and Danny Collins, Deirdre and Jimmy Collins, Julie Sellers, James Fuller, Joey Anderson, Jay Stillman, Dee Hein, Mary Graham, Elizabeth Grantham, John and Wanda Davidson, Saryah Garrison, Mari Velin.

To Tanja, Reannon, Nora, I take space to especially give thanks to you for dedicating so much of yourselves to enrich my life in the way that you do. You have gone beyond the role of job and expectation to bless my life with your own and I certainly can't even hope to honor you the way I should for the impact you've played upon my life.

To Cynthia Rose and Michael Young, for carrying and upholding vision for so long, being the necessary proof to myself and others that indeed It was not we who were crazy but those walking asleep in rest of the world. You were the channel for my first sweat when I started opening to higher 'conscious' so long ago.

To Moonwater and Thunder Strikes, the Deer Tribe Medicine Society, Twisted Hair Elders, and all wisdom keepers across the globe, for teaching the traditions, wheels within wheels, ceremonies, rituals, and ways of aligning self to Creation and Spirit through sweat lodges, Sundance, and various ceremony.

To the Heartwood Institute of Healing Arts family, Bruce and Chela Berger, Gayna Uransky, Nirmalo and all the others who touched my heart there; thank you each for creating, fostering, and holding such a beautiful and sacred space for people to come together, congregate, learn, experience, and dream from each other the teachings which will assist in turning tide in the times ahead. I felt more at home here than anywhere else I had been in all my travels.

For all my kind friends at the Shepherd Center, who have aided me with all the things that have lead me this far, I cannot say thanks enough and this certainly does not suffice. You are doing incredible work saving lives and family, your dharma will be your reward. To the Shepherd's for starting the center, Minna Hong, who is and has been the kindest supporter of my work and illustration of 'moving on' for countless others, Mark Johnson and Carol Jones, for inspiring me by example to have hope that things can change and for leading charge, letting everyone else know that we are each responsible for the state of our world, Pam Mcclure, for being such a kind friend and creating avenues for me to share my work, Bob Baird, for managing the budgets and supervising progress, development of wheelchair sports in this country, Rebecca Washburn, Joy Burns, entire TR staff - all the occupational, physical, recreational therapists, all Doctors- Leslie, Bowman, Apple, Killorin; Nurses everyone especially Shirley Millwood, Amy, Jeane Gaothorsen-, Seating Clinic, Robert Meahan, David Kruetz; all staff, everybody there, thank you all for all you do, your kindness will be your reward.

To the people of the Roosevelt Warm Springs Institute for Rehabilitation and Options Cottage, Thankful I am for your service and nurturance, supporting the Independent Living Philosophy. You gave me space early on in my disability to redefine myself, values and goals and also the time to finish my second book 'When the evening Dies'- Jim Carrell, Darby McCamy, Mike Means and all the aides.

To Disability Connections for all the great work you do in the middle Georgia area, thanks for supporting me as an advocate when I first got involved in ADAPT and for allowing me to do it my own way- Jerilyn and Mike Leverett and rest of supporting cast including Mark Dyer and Andreena Patton.

To all the advocates of the Statewide Independent Living Center, Pat Puckett, the Governor's Council on Developmental Disability, Marcy Dolgoff and Iris Mcilvaine, Unlock the Waiting Lists, Beth Tumlin, Disability Link, Bernard Baker, Renee Peak, Leonard Roscoe and Judy Sexton of CCSP.

Thanks to Tom Glennon for getting me involved with social work and Programs in Leadership Service degree with Mercer University, allowing me to do ADAPT as my class project and involvement with community. To AmeriCorps and the many girls that worked with me there, aiding me in my independence, thanks kindly, I hold you all in kind regard, Marla Smith, Jenny Cribb, for aiding when I had but 3 ½ hours of support. Thanks also to Christy Yarbrough and DS Medical.

Thanks to Disabled Dealer Magazine, for allowing me to share my thoughts and concerns with audience since 1997 in a monthly column called 'Keeping you Connected...' I owe you much more than just the exposure, writing for you has forced an evolution in my word, ways of thinking, and portraying thought when nothing else would have- Cynthia Kimball, Cee Cee Ryan, and the All-In- Ones for introducing me to them.

Honor to ADAPT and Not Dead Yet for not
allowing government to get away with not doing
what is right for the people; the leadership posse-
Bob Kafka, Stephanie Thomas, Mike Auberger,
Babs Johnson, Mike Oxford, Mark Johnson, Linda
Anthony, Diane Coleman, Lou Ann Kibee, Barbara
Toomer, LaTonya Reeves, Rick James, Gil Casarez,
Dawn Russell, Anita Cameron, Roland Sykes,
Kathleen Kleinman, Gayle Hafner, Crosby King,
Marva Ways, Michelle Stieger, Mary O'Brien,
Tony Perrone, Zan Thornton, Scott Heinzman,
Claude Holcombe, Bob Liston, Marsha Katz,
Nadina LaSpina, Shona and Mike Eakin, Jimmi
Schrode, Erik von Shmetterling, the Glozier's,
Frank Lozano, Alfredo Juarez, and supporting cast.

For all my friends at Calle Vinas, I say thank you
for myself and countless others. To Tracy Simpson,
I honor you my dear friend for all you've done for
me, I can only hope to further our friendship with
many new memories and laughter. To Jimmy
Selph, I honor you for supporting my ideas and
believing in me when many didn't. It has turned
out to be a beautiful dream, who knows how many
will be helped by the services Calle Vinas provides.
To supporting cast for all you do, much, much love
and praise- Margaret Selph, Jules Prough, Norma
Smith, Melody Battle, Sarah Chesley, Angie Phelts
and rest of staff. Angie, I hope we get to be great
friends, who knows where future may lead.

Thanks to Dr. Ron Richards for easing my pain,
Janel Bramlett, and Lacie Martin for their comedic
company, never are they a dull moment.

To Dominic Ottaviano and Sandi Simpson, thanks for being involved in all my endeavors, and for listening, trusting that I know what I am talking about when I sometimes do and for giving me shit when I sometimes don't. We've had great times.

To Lacy and Company for always supporting my endeavors, worrying about my health, being more than case workers and more like life supporters, friends Carolyn Lacy, Nannette Armstrong, and Bylinda Byron.

To the American Wheelchair Fencing Team, coach – Maestro Janusz Mylnarz; fellow athletes, friends; Carol Hickey, Kris Alexander, Roy Day, Pete Collman, Curtis Lovejoy, Tony Boatright, Benjy Williams, Scott Rodgers, Lisa Lanier, Jo Ann Stoup, Vicki Bullard, Mark and Carey Calhoun, Gary van DerWege, Gerard Moreno, Susan Gilmore, Sean Shumate, Steven Sikorsky, and Mario Rodriguez. I can't say enough of how much being part of this team and having combat in my life again has filled me so. There's nothing like representing the USA in sport and goal. Great luck to my team this year in Athens, Greece.

To the fencing volunteers who have stuck it out over the years making our practices and tournaments possible, so much thanks to you both- Audra Morabito and Brock Feathers.

To my cats Patchouilli and Morrison, for all the great laughs, entertainment, and unconditional love seldom displayed so graciously among humankind.

To my friends and the Professors at the University of Georgia Exercise Science Department for allowing my involvement in the various studies, research in muscle development post-injury.

Thanks to Dr. Walton, and all the nurses at Athens Regional- for saving my life and caring for people the way you do. I love all of you whom without this book would never have even been possible.

To Tom Olin, thanks man for the great photos, friendship, and allowing me to showcase your work in this way. I hope it does credit to your strive for excellence and quality in your own art.

Thanks to other authors and photographers, who have allowed me to involve their work with my own. I can only hope that this book does justice to the themes you have elected to bring out in your own lives, the Buddha, Lao Tzu, Gandhi, William Blake, Jim Morrison, Neale Donald Walsch and The Humanities Team, Carlos Castaneda, Wesley J. Smith, Ram Dass, Diane Coleman, Sandi Simpson, Dominic Ottaviano, George Weld, and Melinda Beasley.

Finally but especially not least, I thank the people and legislations that make the Independent Care Waiver, Brain and Spinal Cord Injury, and other grants possible. To those who bring these services into our homes and make life such the blessing that it is, so many like myself are indebted to your kind service. And so from all of us, THANK YOU.

-Tom Olin

I lay claim to nothing
exclusively divine in me.
I do not claim prophet ship.
I am but a humble seeker after Truth
and bent upon finding it.
I count no sacrifice too great
for the sake of seeing
God face to face.
The whole of my activity
whether it may be called
social, political, humanitarian or ethical
is directed to that end.
And as I know that God
is found more often
in the lowliest of His creatures
than in the high and mighty,
I am struggling
to reach the status of these.
I cannot do so
without their service.
Hence my passion for the service
of the suppressed classes.
And I cannot render this service
without entering politics,
I find myself in them.
Thus I am no master,
I am but a struggling,
erring, humble servant
of India
and, there through, of humanity.

-Gandhi

About The Author:

-Sandi Simpson

Zen Garcia is a 33 year old, single parent, born August 19th, 1970 at 2:37 p.m. He resides independently in Winder, Georgia, where he spends most of his time advocating, writing, fencing, reading, and drawing.

He had been attending massage school at the Heartwood Institute of Healing arts when he was injured on September 24th, 1994, hitchhiking to a Grateful Dead show in San Francisco, California.

A Different Way Of Being represents his 3rd published manuscript. The first two, Look Somewhere Different and When The Evening Dies... are available through Amazon.com.

He is a member of ADAPT, NOT DEAD YET, The Humanity's Team and the Shepherd Blades; the largest North American Wheelchair Fencing Team currently established.

He publishes a monthly 1500 word column called "Keeping You Connected" through the Disabled Dealer Magazine Of The Southeast.

Sources Cited:

The author gratefully acknowledges the following works:

The Active Side Of Infinity by Carlos Castaneda. Copyright©1998 by Laugan Productions. Published by HarperPerennial, a division of HarperCollins.

Gandhi: All men are Brothers. Autobiographical Reflections by Gandhi. Copyright©1997 by The Continuum Publishing Company.

The American Night by Jim Morrison. Copyright©1990 by Wilderness Publications. Published by Villard Books, a division of Random House, Inc.

Still Here: Embracing Aging, Changing, and Dying by Ram Dass, Marlene Roeder (Ed.), and Mark Matousek. Copyright©2000 by Riverhead Books.

Conversations With God (Books 2) by Neale Donald Walsch. Copyright© 1997. Hampton Roads Publishing Company, Inc.

Communion With God by Neale Donald Walsch. Copyright©2000 by Neale Donald Walsch. Published by G.P. Putnam's Sons, a division of Penguin Putnam, Inc.

We are beings
on our way to dying, he said.
We are not immortal,
but we behave as if we were.
This is the flaw
that brings us down as individuals
and will bring us down
as a species some day.
A shaman's advantage
over their average fellow men
is that shaman's know
they are beings on their way to dying
and they don't
let themselves deviate
from that knowledge.
Someday I'll tell you more
about the forces that drive a man
to act like an ass.

-Carlos Castaneda